AMERICAN E
STANDING COMMITTEE ON

Experts Debate the USA PATRIOT Act

Stewart A. Baker and John Kavanagh
Editors

With an introduction by ABA President Robert J. Grey

AMERICAN BAR ASSOCIATION
Defending Liberty
Pursuing Justice

Cover design by ABA Publishing

This publication was produced with the generous support of the Dr. Scholl Foundation.

09 08 07 06 05   5 4 3

Cataloging-in-Publication data is on file with the Library of Congress

Baker, Stewart A.

Patriot debates / Stewart A. Baker, editor
    ISBN 1-59031-537-5

Discounts are available for books ordered in bulk. Special consideration is given to state bars, CLE programs, and other bar-related organizations. Inquire at Book Publishing, ABA Publishing, American Bar Association, 321 North Clark Street, Chicago, Illinois 60610.

www.ababooks.org

Table of Contents

Introduction

ABA President Robert J. Grey, Jr.

I n keeping with the finest traditions of the American Bar Association, I am pleased to introduce the following series of essays regarding the USA PATRIOT Act and related topics. Later this year, the Congress will determine whether the provisions of the Act that are due to expire at the end of 2005 should be renewed. The ABA believes that an intensive review and thorough civil discourse on the provisions of the Act should precede the congressional vote.

Pursuant to ABA Section on Individual Rights and Responsibilities Report Nos. 112B and 118, the ABA passed resolutions urging the Congress "to conduct a thorough review of the implementation of the powers granted to the Executive Branch under the [USA PATRIOT] Act before considering legislation that would extend or further expand such powers . . ." and "to conduct regular and timely oversight including public hearings . . . to ensure that government investigations undertaken pursuant to the Foreign Intelligence Surveillance Act . . . do not violate the First, Fourth, and Fifth Amendments of the Constitution. . . ."

As Congress prepares for that review and oversight this year, the ABA is delighted to contribute to and promote public debate through the publication of this series of "point" and "counterpoint" essay exchanges.

I extend my congratulations to the Standing Committee on Law and National Security and its chairman, Stewart Baker, for assembling some of the brightest minds in national security and privacy law for this important effort.

Preface

Deputy Attorney General James B. Comey

L ots of words have been spilled over the PATRIOT Act, in many different forums. We spill more here. And although sparing trees is a worthy cause, we further another important cause with the publication of this series—to inform the public about a critical step our Congress took when it overwhelmingly passed the PATRIOT Act, in the wake of the horrific attacks of September 11, 2001. Simply, the PATRIOT Act bolsters our law enforcement and intelligence capabilities and better protects America against senseless terrorist violence. It is an important and worthy Act, and so it is appropriate to debate and understand it, to get beyond bumper stickers to a genuine understanding of a complicated Act.

To my dismay, it has seeped into the nation's drinking water that the PATRIOT Act requires a trade-off between civil liberties and privacy on the one hand, and the protection of national security, on the other hand. I reject that. The men and women of the Department of Justice do great work and care passionately about the civil liberties and freedoms of our fellow Americans. The PATRIOT Act, which we use and enforce, requires no such trade-off. It allows us to serve and to protect, to borrow a phrase, and it is fully consistent with our reverence for civil liberties and individual freedoms. Why? Built into the PATRIOT Act, by our Congress, are numerous protections that ought to give great comfort to all citizens.

Some of those protections are misunderstood or overlooked, but they are very much in place. For instance, to execute a search and then delay notification to the target of that search—something law enforcement has long been able to do when the facts justify it —the FBI must first apply to a federal judge and obtain permission. The same holds true if the FBI wants to conduct roving electronic surveillance or to obtain records under the PATRIOT Act's business records provision.

At the same time that federal judges are looking over one shoulder, the Congress is looking over our other shoulder. We are required to report to the Congress at regular intervals on our use of these—and other—provisions of the PATRIOT Act. That is healthy and proper, and helps ensure that we use these important tools in a responsible manner, consonant with the civil liberties we hold so dear. Within the Department of Justice, our Inspector General is also required, by the terms of the Act, to monitor our use of the PATRIOT Act, and receive and investigate allegations of abuse.

Good lawyers never shy from debates, and this is a particularly good time to debate this important act. Some of the most important provisions of the PATRIOT Act are due to expire at the end of this year, so we ought to be talking and writing and thinking about it every chance we get. With respect to the PATRIOT Act, the angel—not the devil—is in the details. If all participants in the discussion demand those details and move beyond slogans to an understanding of how these tools are used, and why they matter so much, our country will be well served.

Enjoy the words of the wise men and women who have contributed to this discussion and to this series.

Editors' Introduction

Stewart Baker

John Kavanagh

I t is now three and a half years since the September 11 attacks, and almost that long since the USA PATRIOT Act was adopted. For comparison purposes, in the three and a half years after Pearl Harbor, the United States crossed the Pacific, retook the Philippines, landed on Iwo Jima, and also crossed the Atlantic, the English Channel, and the Rhine. The war in Europe was essentially over, and the war in the Pacific had only a few months to run.

Measured by that standard, the eventful years since September 11, 2001, don't seem quite so dramatic. But they do make the three-and-a-half-year mark an appropriate time to evaluate the global war on terror and the tools we've used to wage it. The USA PATRIOT Act has been a part of that effort, and this compilation of essays is the beginning of the evaluation.

Many provisions of the USA PATRIOT Act will expire at the end of 2005. This book is devoted to civil and informed debate about these provisions and whether they should be renewed, as well as a few other issues that are likely to be part of the renewal debate in 2005. We have an all-star cast of contributors from both sides of the debate, and the Standing Committee's effort to spark a civil, tough debate about the USA PATRIOT Act is already paying dividends. For starters, it's becoming clear that large parts of the Act, and many of the provisions due to sunset, are nowhere near as controversial as the Act's press coverage might suggest. In several cases, the civil libertarians we recruited to find fault with particular provisions have ended up proposing modification rather than repeal. And for other provisions, we couldn't find anyone who wanted to argue against renewal.

That doesn't mean we lack for controversy or deeply felt divisions. But it does mean that the debate over USA PATRIOT may boil down to a handful of sunsetting provisions—some of which are not serious candidates for repeal as much as for revision—and a variety of other issues spurred not by the sunset requirement but by a general desire to clean up some of the loose ends in the legal war on terror now that we have three and a half years of struggle behind us.

The contributors whom we have gathered for this series of debates are among the most eloquent voices in their field. We thank the authors for their time and contributions. We have attempted to capture the essence of their essays in the paragraphs below and hope to entice readers to turn quickly to the full debates.

Section 203

Perhaps the bravest of our contributors is Kate Martin, who agreed to make the case against section 203, the provision that authorizes information sharing between law enforcement and intelligence agencies. This was uncontroversial when USA PATRIOT was adopted, but Kate Martin argues that the legal barriers to sharing between agencies have been overrated as a cause of the intelligence failures before 9/11. She isn't prepared to argue for wholesale repeal of the provision, but she would require a second court order before data moves from the law enforcement world to the intelligence world and would put strict limits on what kinds of information can be moved across that boundary.

Viet Dinh returns to the arguments that got section 203 enacted—the need to abolish all excuses for a lack of information sharing about terrorism between agencies. And he says that section 203 contains statutory restrictions that, when combined with Attorney General guidelines, provide plenty of privacy protection.

Kate Martin's reply yields no ground, challenging Viet Dinh to show what barriers existed before section 203 and arguing that existing protections are illusory.

Section 206

Like Kate Martin's treatment of section 203, Jim Dempsey's criticism of section 206 falls into the "mend it, don't end it" school.

rule"). He would not get rid of the provision, but he would restrict searches of library records, impose a higher standard for section 215 orders, and cut back the gag rule.

These two essayists may be our best-matched pair. They like to mix it up, and they do it well. Even so, when we tried to spark a fight over a separate provision, section 214, we were unable to create much controversy. Andrew McCarthy defends it as an "eminently reasonable" modification of the rules for obtaining a pen register when investigating an agent of a foreign power. Peter Swire suggests that the standard may have been set too low. But no one wants to waste much firepower on the section.

Section 218

Section 218 allows national security wiretaps when foreign intelligence is "a significant purpose"—as opposed to the primary purpose of the tap. Before 9/11, the Justice Department was haunted by fear that a national security tap would be declared unlawful because the government's purpose had shaded across the line between intelligence and prosecution. This amendment was meant to move the line and allow more cooperation between law enforcement and intelligence agencies. Andrew McCarthy ably sets forth this history, including the appellate decision that greatly eased the government's primary purpose worries, not long after Congress had enacted section 218. Going back to the primary-purpose test after all that history, he argues, would be a disaster.

David Cole is as brave as Kate Martin in arguing that section 218 did not eliminate the wall that contributed to the intelligence failures before 9/11. He blames bureaucratic barriers, not the primary-purpose test, for a lack of information sharing, which he says was perfectly legal under the old rules. If the purpose of a wiretap migrates into criminal territory, he argues, then the government can always get a criminal wiretap order and continue as before. In fact, it has to, according to David Cole, because that's what the Constitution requires.

Intercepting Lone Wolf Terrorists

Long after USA PATRIOT, Congress amended FISA's wiretap standards as part of a bill enacting the 9/11 Commission's reform package. The amendment makes it easier to wiretap terrorists without tying them conclusively to a particular group or nation. The change arises out of the Moussaoui mess. FBI agents thought that they had to link Moussaoui to a particular terrorist group in order to get a FISA warrant to search his computer. The lone wolf provision makes clear that such ties aren't required.

Michael Woods defends the provision by arguing that other aspects of FISA provide an assurance that the law cannot be used against domestic terrorists. That's because FISA still requires an international element to any terrorists subject to intercept under that Act.

Suzanne Spaulding thinks the amendment was unnecessary—the FBI misunderstood the law in the *Moussaoui* case—and is likely to undermine FISA's constitutional standing by moving too far from the military and foreign affairs focus that takes FISA out of the normal Fourth Amendment rubric.

Borders

Control of U.S. borders is not formally an issue raised by the expiration of some parts of USA PATRIOT. But it is almost certain to be part of the debate, given the support in the House for the "REAL I.D. Act" sponsored by Rep. Sensenbrenner. George Terwilliger urges aggressive legal action to control illegal immigration. He supports a national identity card, an approach to applicants for entry that differentiates by likely threat, an end to the release of asylum claimants while their cases are pending, the exclusion of illegal immigrants, with jail terms for repeat offenders, and the fingerprinting of all foreign visitors and immigrants.

Tim Edgar is appalled. He attacks the REAL I.D. Act, noting that it wouldn't have stopped the 9/11 hijackers, and condemns as ineffective and counterproductive any effort to identify likely terrorists by ethnic or other measures.

Detainees

Detainees aren't formally on the USA PATRIOT agenda either. But detainee issues have spurred much of the judicial lawmaking on terrorism since 9/11. And Congress may need to shore up the Executive's eroding strategy for detaining potentially dangerous people. Calls for Congress to enact an American "preventive detention" law have come from unexpected quarters. Patricia Wald and Joe Onek are skeptical about preventive detention—and about most of the other detention mechanisms invoked in the weeks after 9/11. They would like to see a ban on using the material witness statute as a holding device unconnected to imminent testimony.

John Yoo and Gregory Jacob defend the Administration's record on detentions, finding comfort even in recent Supreme Court cases. They liken the use of material witness laws to Robert Kennedy's pledge to prosecute mobsters for a variety of crimes, including "spitting on the sidewalk." Wald and Onek respond that the definition of "enemy combatant" should be limited to an enemy soldier or a person captured on the battlefield and engaged in armed conflict against the United States. Yoo and Jacob object that even the Geneva Convention defines "enemy combatant" more broadly.

Material Support to Terrorist Organizations

The USA PATRIOT Act expanded an existing ban on providing "material support or resources" to organizations designated as "foreign terrorist" groups by the Secretary of State. The Intelligence Reform Act further elaborated on the provision. Although this provision is not scheduled for sunset, David Cole thinks that a ban on providing "expert advice or assistance" is unconstitutional and a likely source of serious First Amendment abuses. He relies heavily on Supreme Court cases from the 1950s that protected Communist Party members from "guilt by association" to argue that such assistance can only be unlawful if the donor intends or knows that the gift will assist terrorist acts.

Paul Rosenzweig wonders what all the fuss is about. The provisions have been around a long while and the claimed abuses haven't materialized. Any help to a terrorist organization is suspect, he says, even aid to humanitarian activities, since this just frees up other resources for terror attacks. As for vagueness and overbreadth, he argues, the statute is clear enough and has not been systematically abused despite the overwrought claims on the left.

Part One
Provisions Expiring in 2005

Section 203.
Authority to Share Criminal Investigative Information

Kate Martin
Viet Dinh

Summary

Mary DeRosa

Section 203 authorizes sharing of "foreign intelligence" information gathered in criminal investigations with certain federal officials. Only subsections 203(b) and 203(d) are subject to the PATRIOT Act's sunset provision. Section 203(b) amends federal wiretap law to permit law enforcement officials to disclose wiretap contents to any other "federal law enforcement, intelligence, protective, immigration, national defense, or national security official" to the extent the information contains "foreign intelligence," "counterintelligence," or "foreign intelligence information" and will assist the official in performance of his or her duties. Section 203(d) contains a more general authority for sharing the same types of information, when it is obtained in criminal investigations, with the same types of officials under the same circumstances. It also authorizes disclosure of threat information collected in a criminal investigation to "appropriate" federal, state, local, or foreign government officials for the purpose of responding to that threat. Threat information can include threat of attack, other "grave hostile acts," sabotage, terrorism, or clandestine intelligence-gathering activities.

Section 203 borrows its definition of "foreign intelligence" and "counterintelligence" from the National Security Act of 1947. The term "foreign intelligence information" is new; it is defined to include information about U.S. Persons and covers information that (a) relates to the ability of the United States to protect against ac-

3

tual or potential attack, sabotage, terrorism, or clandestine intelligence activities of a foreign power, or (b) with respect to a foreign power, relates to "the national defense or security of the United States" or "the conduct of the foreign affairs of the United States."

Section 203 was designed to address the concern that there were barriers to information sharing between law enforcement and national security officials. A different section of the Act, section 905, which does not sunset, requires the Attorney General or heads of other law enforcement agencies to disclose "foreign intelligence" from criminal investigations to the Director of Central Intelligence (subsequent legislation substituted the new Director of National Intelligence for the DCI).

Kate Martin

Why Sections 203 and 905 Should Be Modified

Three different sections of the PATRIOT Act authorize and require the sharing of information collected on Americans by one government agency with a wide range of officials in many other government agencies. Since the passage of the PATRIOT Act, Congress has also required the sharing of information in the Enhanced Border Security and Visa Entry Reform Act and the Homeland Security Act and ordered the construction of vast new information-sharing technologies.

While effective counterterrorism requires that agencies share relevant information, congressional efforts have uniformly failed to address the real difficulties in such sharing: how to determine what information is useful for counterterrorism; how to determine what information would be useful if shared; how to identify whom it would be useful to share it with; and how to ensure that useful and relevant information is timely recognized and acted upon. To the contrary, the legislative approach—which can fairly be summarized as share everything with everyone—can be counted on to obscure and make more difficult the real challenge of information sharing.

Widespread and indiscriminate warehousing of information about individuals violates basic privacy principles. Amending the PATRIOT Act to require targeted rather than indiscriminate information sharing would restore at least minimal privacy protections and substantially increase the likelihood that the government could identify and obtain the specific information needed to prevent terrorist acts.

Pre-9/11 Intelligence Failures

The PATRIOT Act's information-sharing provisions have been touted as a response to the pre-9/11 intelligence failures, but those failures were not due to legal barriers, and the provisions in the Act do not fix the problems that led to the 9/11 failures.

Contrary to the repeated mischaracterization by Attorney General Ashcroft and others, no statutory "wall" prohibited sharing information between the law enforcement and intelligence communities; the law expressly provided for such sharing. While the Foreign Intelligence Surveillance Act (FISA) was interpreted to mean that prosecutors could not direct foreign intelligence wiretaps, as opposed to criminal wiretaps, the text of FISA expressly contemplates that FISA surveillance may uncover evidence of a crime. Before September 11, FISA information had been used in many criminal cases. While there were statutory restrictions on sharing some secret grand jury information or criminal wiretap intercepts with the CIA or the White House, those rules had exceptions when national security was at stake. *See, e.g.*, August 14, 1997, Memorandum to the Acting Counsel, and October 17, 2000, Memorandum to the Counsel, Office of Intelligence Policy and Review.

Moreover, none of the 9/11 failures was caused by the inability of prosecutors to direct FISA surveillance, or any legal restriction on the CIA or White House obtaining secret grand jury or wiretap information. The reports of the Congressional Joint Inquiry and 9/11 Commission describe many missed opportunities in detail. Nowhere do they identify any statutory prohibition

5

on information sharing as at fault, although there were widespread bureaucratic misunderstandings about legal restrictions on information sharing.

Instead, the failures resulted from the FBI and CIA failing to know what it knew. For example, while lower-level FBI agents had important information about Al Qaeda associates in the United States that they shared with Headquarters, the higher-ups failed to understand the significance of the information, much less act on it. Similarly, the CIA knew for almost two years about the U.S. visa issued to an Al Qaeda suspect—who would hijack a plane on September 11— but failed to inform the FBI or appreciate the importance of the information. This was a failure of analysis and coordination; it was not caused by legal restrictions on access to information.

The PATRIOT Act

Rather than analyze and grapple with the real causes of the 9/11 failures, Congress in the PATRIOT Act simply required indiscriminate sharing of information without addressing the problem of how to identify and analyze important information. The PATRIOT Act provisions make that task more difficult by deluging agencies with unanalyzed and often irrelevant information.

Section 203 of the Act allows the unrestricted sharing of sensitive information gathered by law enforcement agencies with the CIA, the NSA, immigration authorities, the Secret Service, and White House officials. It does not limit such sharing to officials with responsibility for terrorism matters, nor are there any safeguards regarding the subsequent use or dissemination of such information by such officials (so long as the use is within the official duties of the recipient). It allows the sharing of all information that is in any way related to any American's contacts with or activities involving any foreign government, group, or individual. It applies to all intercepts of telephone conversations and e-mail. It applies to all confidential information obtained by a grand jury, which has the power, merely at the request of a prosecutor, to subpoena virtually any records and any testimony from any person. A key safeguard against this virtually unlimited subpoena power had been the requirement that grand jury information only be shared for legitimate law enforcement purposes under the supervision of a judge.

Section 905 overlaps with section 203 but makes such sharing mandatory. It requires the Attorney General and the head of any other law enforcement agency to "expeditiously disclose" to the Director of Central Intelligence (and now the new Director of National Intelligence) all "foreign intelligence" acquired during a law enforcement investigation. The Attorney General may exempt only those classes of foreign intelligence whose disclosure "would jeopardize an ongoing law enforcement investigation or impair other significant law enforcement interests." Section 905 suffers from the same defects as section 203: it covers the most sensitive grand jury information and wiretap intercepts regardless of relevance, and contains no limits on the use or redisclosure of the information by intelligence agency staff. "Foreign intelligence" includes anything related to any American's contacts with a foreign government, group or person. Over the objections of civil liberties groups and some Democratic senators, the administration refused to limit this mandatory sharing to information related to international terrorism or to limit it to intelligence officials with counterterrorism responsibilities. The Act sets no standards or safeguards for use of this information. While it requires the Attorney General to issue rules, those rules simply require that information concerning citizens and legal permanent residents be marked as such and contain no limitations or safeguards on the use of the information.

Section 504 of the Act makes explicit that FISA information may be shared with law enforcement personnel. This provision—proposed by Senator Leahy, not the Administration—alone would have addressed whatever confusion existed about the FISA requirements at the FBI and elsewhere.

The PATRIOT Act and subsequent legislation also vastly expanded the universe of personal information that may now be indiscriminately shared. Section 215, for example, authorizes secret seizures of commercial databases as well as library and other personal records simply on the assertion that they are sought for an authorized investigation.

Notably, the PATRIOT Act nowhere addresses the CIA's failure to share information with other agencies, even though the CIA's failure to alert other agencies that known Al Qaeda associates were coming to the U.S. when it knew Al Qaeda was planning another attack was a major "missed opportunity." Of course, it is not easy to figure out how to ensure that CIA information is shared with other agencies that need it and at the same time protect the confidentiality of truly sensitive intelligence sources. The suggestion that the source of the information should simply be eliminated when distributing the information misunderstands the importance of knowing at least something about the source of information in order to understand the context and reliability of the information. The PATRIOT Act diverts attention from solving these difficult problems by adopting a vacuum cleaner approach to information sharing.

Two and a half years after the passage of the PATRIOT Act, the 9/11 Commission staff confirmed that "there is no national strategy for sharing information to counter terrorism." The Administration has yet to explain how these PATRIOT Act provisions will focus the bureaucracies on identifying what information is useful to locate actual terrorists, analyzing that information, and determining what actions to take based on the information. To the contrary, the provisions essentially direct agencies simply to dump massive volumes of unanalyzed information on other agencies. They facilitate the construction of a vast intelligence database on Americans. And they effect an extraordinary change in the capability and authority of the foreign intelligence agencies, including the CIA, to keep information on Americans.

Fixes

Congress should amend both sections 203 and 905 to provide some simple privacy safeguards, which will also ensure that information sharing is done in a more effective way.

Section 203: Authority to Share Criminal Investigative Information

1. When information is gathered pursuant to judicial power, the court's approval should be required before transferring the information to intelligence agencies, White House personnel, or other law enforcement agencies in order to ensure that there is some real need for more widely distributing the information. Accordingly, court approval for sharing criminal wiretap intercepts of conversations and e-mail and secret grand jury information should be obtained, except when there is no time to obtain such approval in order to prevent an imminent terrorist act or the flight of a suspect.

2. The information that should be shared with the intelligence agencies, the White House, etc., should be limited to information relevant to terrorism or espionage, rather than all information concerning any foreign contacts, the vast majority of which have nothing to do with terrorism. If the information transferred by law enforcement to the intelligence community were limited to "foreign intelligence information" as that term is defined in the Foreign Intelligence Surveillance Act (rather than the much broader definition in section 203), it would offer some protection against the CIA and others constructing a database on information about the domestic activities of Americans.

3. The information should be shared only with those officials who are directly involved in terrorism investigations or analyses.

4. There should be procedures for marking and safeguarding the information so these limits can be enforced and to protect against the redissemination of the information beyond these limits, much as classified information is marked and stored. Confidential grand jury information should be marked as such, and intercepts of Americans' conversations and e-mails should be marked to prohibit indiscriminate circulation.

Conclusion

One of the most basic protections against government abuses has been the principle that a government agency should only collect information about individuals that it needs for a specific and articulated purpose, should use it only for the purposes for which it was collected, should not keep it any longer than necessary, and should not share it with other government agencies except for very good reasons. The PATRIOT Act violates that principle by adopting the approach that myriad government agencies should collect, share, and maintain forever as much information on as many people as possible. Requiring the minimal protection that the government articulate why specific information could be useful for counterterrorism before widely distributing it would help keep the government focused on the information needed to locate the next attackers, instead of warehousing personal information about millions of Americans.

Viet Dinh

Reply

Passed soon after the terrorist attacks of 9/11, the USA PATRIOT Act is among the most important legislative measures in American history. The Act enables the government to fight what will undoubtedly be a long and difficult war against international terrorism.

The specific terrorist prevention successes enabled by the Act—outlined in numerous public briefings and summarized in two comprehensive reports to Congress—justified the Department of Justice's conclusion that its job in securing the safety of America and her people in the years since September 11 "would have been much more difficult, if not impossibly so, without the USA PATRIOT Act."

That success is attributable not only to the collection of more information on terrorist plots, but also to the smarter use of terrorist information collected by the government. Before the Act, the law sharply limited the ability of law enforcement officers to share information with intelligence personnel—even when both halves were working on the same investigation. Through a series of provisions in the USA PATRIOT Act, Congress removed the legal barriers that created the culture of segregation and distrust among the various bureaucracies engaged in the common fight against terrorism.

The investigation and prosecution of the "Lackawanna Six" illustrates the practical impediments of a culture of segregation. In 2001, six members of an Al Qaeda cell in Lackawanna, New York, traveled to Afghanistan for training at an Al Qaeda-affiliated camp. The investigation originated when FBI officials received a letter alleging the residents' involvement with foreign terrorists and criminal activities. In order to retain the option of using FISA, the FBI determined that the law required establishing two separate, simultaneous investigations: an intelligence investigation concerning terrorist threats, and a criminal investigation involving possible drug crimes. The two squads operated independently in the following months, often prohibited from even standing in the same room during briefings to discuss their respective cases. Thus, investigators on both sides were unable to obtain a complete picture of either the terrorist or the criminal activity.

The USA PATRIOT Act erased the statutory impediment to information sharing and provided the impetus to remove the bureaucratic and cultural barriers to cooperation. In the case of the Lackawanna investigation, law enforcement agents were able to learn from intelligence officials that an individual named in the anonymous letter was an agent of Al Qaeda. Additional information shared between intelligence and law enforcement personnel dramatically expedited the investigation. As a result, five of the six suspects pleaded guilty to providing material support to Al Qaeda, and the sixth pleaded guilty to conducting transactions unlawfully with Al Qaeda.

Among the information-sharing provisions was the Act's amendments to grand jury secrecy rules. If a federal prosecutor learned during grand jury testimony that terrorists were planning to detonate a bomb in Manhattan in the next 30 minutes, Federal Rule of Criminal Procedure 6(e) prevented him from immediately notifying national security officials not directly participating in the investigation. Section 203 of the Act now permits sharing of grand jury information regarding foreign intelligence with federal law enforcement, intelligence, protective, immigration, national defense, and national security personnel. Disclosures under section 203 have been used to support the revocation of visas of suspected terrorists and prevent their reentry into the United States, track terrorists' funding sources, and identify terrorist operatives overseas.

Even the most strident of opponents of the USA PATRIOT Act would not want another terrorist attack to occur because law enforcement and intelligence communities were prevented from talking to each other. If a grand jury investigation uncovers evidence about a foreign terrorist cell, there should be some mechanism for the sharing of this information with the intelligence community.

Section 203, essential as it is, does raise important questions about how we approach law enforcement and domestic intelligence. Congress grappled with these issues and placed restrictions on the use of grand jury information—weighing the need for secrecy in the proceedings with the protection of the citizenry from attack. For instance, the official who receives such information may use it only in the course of his official duties and is subject to the rules regarding the unauthorized disclosure. Thus, only those who need the information to do their job potentially have access to it. In addition, any time grand jury information is shared, the government is required to notify the supervising court and identify the departments that received it.

More important, the USA PATRIOT Act does not permit or require the sharing of all—or even most—grand jury or criminal investigative information with the intelligence community. Section 203 of the Act expressly limits disclosure to foreign intelligence information. The Act defines the term foreign intelligence to include information relating to the ability of the United States to defend itself against terrorism, sabotage, and clandestine intelligence activities of foreign powers, as well as information relating to "national defense" or "the conduct of . . . foreign affairs." Rather than open up all criminal investigations to the intelligence community, the Act appropriately restricts the information to the type necessary to counter a threat from abroad. The vast majority of criminal investigations do not contain such information.

In addition, pursuant to the requirements of the USA PATRIOT Act, the Attorney General established procedures to ensure that the information is used appropriately. These procedures require that law enforcement agents, before disclosure to intelligence agencies, label all information identifying a U.S. person. Moreover, upon receipt of information from law enforcement that identifies a U.S. person, intelligence agencies must handle that information pursuant to specific protocols. These protocols, for example, require that information identifying a U.S. person be deleted from the intelligence information except in specified circumstances.

Those in the privacy advocacy industry, of course, would prefer tighter strictures to sharing of government information. Such ham-fisted obstinacy, however, comes with a cost, in terms of both privacy and efficacy. Preventing government from using information smartly will heighten the need for government to collect information more broadly. And bureaucratic strictures threaten to reconstruct the wall between intelligence and law enforcement. Information sharing must be guided by practical guidelines that simultaneously empower and constrain officials, clearly articulating what is and is not permitted.

Karl Llewellyn once wrote, "Ideals without technique are a mess. But technique without ideals is a menace." As Congress engages in the legislative effort to renew the USA PATRIOT Act, it behooves us to reaffirm the ideals of democracy and freedom and also to discern the techniques necessary to safeguard those ideals against the continuing threat of terrorism.

Kate Martin

Response

Professor Dinh's defense of sections 203 and 905 is long on rhetoric and short on substance. In particular, he fails to respond to

Deputy Attorney General Comey's exhortation to discuss the details of these sections.

First, Professor Dinh makes no case about why the broad new authority in sections 203 and 905 is necessary. Even in his telling of it, the pre-9/11 rules on safeguarding sensitive grand jury information and wiretap intercepts which are amended by section 203, had nothing to do with the investigation of the individuals in Lackawanna. (Section 203 is irrelevant to the issues he identifies: intelligence officials not sharing information with law enforcement and the FBI's misreading of FISA.) Likewise, Professor Dinh's hypothetical grand jury testimony about a bomb in New York was anticipated by the Clinton Justice Department, whose Office of Legal Counsel opined in 1993 and 1997 that under then-existing law, prosecutors would be free to disclose such information to national security officials even without prior judicial approval.

Second, Professor Dinh makes no argument against amending sections 203 and 905 to provide some modest protections. The proposed amendments—limiting shared information to information relating to terrorism, limiting its dissemination to officials working on terrorism, requiring judicial approval, and requiring marking to prevent redissemination—would not interfere with the necessities of counterterrorism. Indeed, Professor Dinh has failed to identify any instances of information sharing that would be prevented if the proposed amendments to sections 203 and 905 were made. Information about suspected terrorists like those in Lackawanna or bomb threats could still be shared.

On the other hand, the current law offers no protections against abuse. While Professor Dinh argues that not all information from criminal investigations may be shared, that is no answer to the fact that too much information will be turned over to the CIA and others, including virtually all information about any American's contacts with any foreigner or foreign group, including humanitarian organizations, for example. While Professor Dinh repeats the Justice Department's misleading claim that intelligence agency protocols require that information about Americans be deleted "except in specified circumstances," those circumstances are in fact so broad as to allow intelligence agencies to keep all information obtained under section 203 or 905. *See* E.O. 12333 section 2.3. Existing rules provide virtually no protection against authorized government compilation of dossiers on millions of Americans and use of those dossiers in intelligence operations.

By dealing seriously with the current authorities allowing the building of massive intelligence databases on any American with foreign contacts, Congress could also accomplish the important task of forcing bureaucracies to identify and focus on information that is actually useful in preventing another attack.

Viet Dinh

An Indispensable Tool in the War on Terror

Section 203 both standardizes and restrains the powers of our men and women in blue, illustrating not the false trade-off between liberty and security presented in Ms. Martin's essays, but their mutual reinforcement. Rolling back this provision would return our country to the culture of separation and bureaucratic segregation that hindered effective terrorist prevention.

Ms. Martin's response underestimates the tools necessary to prevent and detect complex webs of terrorist activity. In particular, her contention that all shared information should be first established as terrorism-related information underscores the very crux of the problem—the full relevance of information is often only apparent after information is shared between criminal and intelligence investigations. You cannot connect the dots before all the dots are even on the drawing board.

Moreover, while prior law provided for some dissemination of information, Ms. Martin fails to note how restrictions were so convoluted that agents frequently hesitated from working openly with other government entities. Section 203 has been widely heralded by investigators for helping to clarify confused interpretations and promote a more coordinated and efficient team approach to counterterrorism. Only recently, FBI Director Mueller testified that section 203 has greatly enhanced the FBI's relationships with state, local, and other federal agencies in the common effort to fight terrorism.

Section 206.
Roving Surveillance Authority Under FISA

James X. Dempsey
Paul Rosenzweig

Summary

Mary DeRosa

Section 206 expands the authority of the Foreign Intelligence Surveillance Court (FISC) by allowing it to order "roving" or multi-point surveillance. Previously, FISA required a separate FISC authorization to tap each device a target used. Technically, the court's order would direct a specific carrier or individual to assist in the surveillance. As a practical matter, this required separate application to the FISC each time a target switched from pay phone to cell phone, e-mail to Blackberry, etc. Now, the court may order surveillance focused on the target, rather than the device he or she is using when "the actions of the target of the application may have the effect of thwarting the identification" of a specific device. This new order does not specify the person who is directed to assist; the government may serve the generic order on individuals or carriers that it identifies.

Section 206 modernizes FISA wiretap authority and brings it closer in line with the criminal wiretap laws, which have permitted roving wiretaps since 1986. The FISA roving authority differs from the criminal wiretap laws, however, in that it does not contain a requirement that the government "ascertain" where the targeted communication will take place before intercepting communications. The criminal wiretap law, 18 U.S.C. section 2518(12), states: "An interception of a communication under [a roving surveillance] order . . . shall not begin until the place where the communication is to be intercepted is ascertained by the person implementing the interception order."

Also, under FISA, the government need not always identify a target to obtain a warrant. FISA section 105(c)(1)(A) requires that an order specify "the identity, if known, or a description of the target of the electronic surveillance." Therefore, with the new roving surveillance authority, the government may obtain an order to conduct surveillance that specifies neither a named target nor a specific device to tap, although the order must provide a description of the target if a name is not known.

James X. Dempsey

Why Section 206 Should Be Modified

Section 206 of the USA PATRIOT Act authorized "roving" wiretaps under the Foreign Intelligence Surveillance Act (FISA). Under this provision, the FBI in an intelligence investigation can obtain a court order to intercept an individual's communications without specifying the particular phone line or computer account to which the interception will apply. Thus, if a suspected spy or terrorist is moving from safehouse to safehouse, or is using public access computers, or is changing cell phones frequently, the FBI can continue to intercept the individual's communications without having to return to court for a new order covering each new phone line or computer.

It makes perfect sense that the FBI should have roving tap authority in intelligence investigations of terrorists. In fact, the FBI had been given roving tap authority in criminal investigations of terrorists in 1986, and there was no good reason why similar authority had not been granted at the same time for intelligence investigations under FISA. During the PATRIOT Act debate, the Justice Department sometimes justified section 206 by claiming that it needed the same authority to investigate dangerous terrorists that it already had for ordinary criminals, but in reality DOJ already did have—prior to the PATRIOT Act—roving tap authority for terrorists plotting attacks or raising money and being investigated under the criminal law.

So, as with so many provisions of the PATRIOT Act, the concern with section 206 is not with the authority itself. Rather, the issue is the lack of adequate checks and balances. Roving taps pose obvious risks. Constitutionally, they are suspect, since they depart from the Fourth Amendment's explicit requirement that all warrants must "particularly describ[e] the place to be searched." Practically, they pose the risk of intercepting the communications of innocent persons, risks that are separate from those addressed by the minimization requirement of the wiretap laws. Congress recognized when it first created the roving tap authority for criminal cases that it needed to add extra procedural protections to overcome the constitutional problems and to guard against the interception of the conversations of innocent people.

However, even though the DOJ argued in the PATRIOT Act debates that it wanted in intelligence investigations of terrorists the same roving tap authority it had for criminal investigations of terrorists, section 206 lacks two important protections that apply to criminal roving taps. The first is the so-called ascertainment requirement—the requirement that agents actually ascertain the location of the suspect before turning on their recording devices. Secondly, some additional changes to FISA adopted outside of the normal process in the Intelligence Authorization Act a few months after the PATRIOT Act had the probably unintended effect of seeming to authorize "John Doe" roving taps—that is, FISA orders that identify neither the target nor the location of the interception.

As a result, a new imbalance has been created, leaving the FBI without appropriate oversight in the use of its roving tap power under FISA and making it more likely that the e-mail and telephone conversations of innocent people will be inadvertently monitored. Fortunately, these are problems that can be fixed without taking away the roving tap authority for intelligence investigations.

First, roving taps in criminal cases are subject to an "ascertainment" requirement. This means that the surveillance can be set up in advance but cannot be activated until the officers in charge of the operation have a good sense that the target is actually using a particular telephone or computer. For example, the roving tap on a hotel room cannot be activated until the suspect checks into the hotel. A roving tap on a computer in a library can be all set up but it cannot be activated until the suspect is seen to sit down at the particular computer. This ascertainment requirement helps ensure that a wiretap is turned on only when the target is present, and thereby protects the privacy of innocent users. The FISA roving tap authority added by the PATRIOT Act has no parallel protection.

This can be fixed pretty easily: an ascertainment requirement should be added to the FISA roving tap authority in 50 U.S.C. section 1805(c) to require that "in cases where the facility or place at which the surveillance is to be directed is not known at the time the order is issued, the surveillance be conducted only when the presence of the target at a particular facility or place has been ascertained by the person conducting the surveillance."

This language was proposed in the SAFE Act, a bipartisan bill introduced in the 108th Congress as H.R. 3352 and S. 1709 and expected to be reintroduced in the 109th Congress. It is based directly on the ascertainment requirement for roving bugs in criminal cases, which requires that the interception "shall not begin until the place where the communication is to be intercepted is ascertained by the person implementing the interception order." 18 U.S.C. § 2518(12). That standard is clearer than the ascertainment requirement currently provided for roving phone taps in criminal cases, which was rewritten a number of years ago without much forethought and no longer makes much sense.

Second, as to the John Doe issue, the rule for FISA taps should be the same as the rule for criminal taps, which is very simple: the government's application and the judicial warrant should specify either the person or the place to be surveilled. *See* 18 U.S.C. §

2518(11)(b)(ii), in the criminal wiretap statute, which specifically requires that a roving tap must "identif[y] the person" to be tapped. However, as a result of changes made "outside the scope" of the FY 2002 intelligence authorization bill conference, FISA as now drafted seems to allow applications and orders that specify neither the person nor the location to be tapped. Specifically, the statute permits the FISA court to issue an order that specifies "the identity, if known, or a description of the target of the electronic surveillance" and "the nature and location of each of the facilities or places at which the electronic surveillance will be directed, if known." 50 U.S.C. § 1805(c)(1)(A), (B). The roving tap authority, which was added in a somewhat careless fashion, does not require roving taps to specifically identify the target of the surveillance. Thus, if neither the identity nor the facilities are known, the order could be issued with only a general description of the individual to be tapped. Neither the statute nor the legislative history indicates how specific any such description must be.

This is unprecedented, probably unintended, and probably unconstitutional. It permits the FISA court to issue a wiretap order authorizing the FBI to listen in on a telephone or e-mail conversation of a person not named in the order, at any telephone or computer the unnamed person might use. This loophole, even if it was unintentional, should be corrected. A simple change that clarifies that a FISA wiretap order must specify either the target or the facility—but not neither—would remedy this problem and should not be controversial. Again, the bipartisan SAFE Act addressed this issue, adding language to 50 U.S.C. section 1805(c)(1) making it clear that, if the identity of the target is unknown, the facilities and places shall be specified, or, if the facilities or places where the surveillance is to be conducted are unknown, the identity of the target shall be specified.

The Justice Department has already admitted that a roving tap order must include a "description" of the target. *See* Letter from John Ashcroft to Sen. Orrin Hatch, at 2-3 (Jan. 28, 2004). But "description" is not defined in FISA and DOJ has failed to offer an adequate definition of its own. Is "20- to 35-year-old Arab male" an adequate description? It describes thousands of people in the United States. On the other hand, if a description is an alias or is so detailed that it could reasonably describe only one person, then that description surely could be considered an "identity," permitting a roving tap to be employed.

This problem should be corrected legislatively. Clear legislative definitions are particularly important in FISA, because the role of the courts in defining the limits of the statute is much more constrained. Title III, in contrast to FISA, requires notice after the fact to all targets of surveillance. This means that persons mistakenly surveilled can meaningfully challenge the government's actions. Under FISA, the government normally never notifies targets that they have been wiretapped. Even in cases where FISA-gathered evidence is used in a criminal proceeding, the normal adversarial rules have not been applied. No defendant has ever gotten access to the underlying FISA application and order, thereby severely hampering his ability to challenge the legality of the search.

Like so many of the controversial surveillance provisions of the PATRIOT Act, Section 206 took an otherwise valid idea a step too far. Extending roving taps to intelligence investigations was not in itself a substantial civil liberties problem. But authorizing roving intelligence taps without sufficient safeguards is.

Paul Rosenzweig

Terrorism Is Not Just a Crime

Shortly after the PATRIOT Act was passed, opponents of the Act wrote of section 206: "These wiretaps pose a greater challenge to privacy because they are authorized secretly without a showing of probable cause of crime . . . This Section represents a broad expansion of power without building in a necessary privacy protection." Thus was painted an apocalyptic picture of Big Brother on steroids—a security apparatus that can listen to "anyone at any time."

Fortunately, the discussion of section 206 that we are engaged in here is a far more measured and thoughtful one of nuance. We are agreed, as I understand it, that the extension, generally, of roving wiretap authority to intelligence investigations is wise, and our disagreements, such as they are, exist at the margins.

It is useful, before addressing those disagreements, to recall the genesis of the roving wiretap rules and the fundamental reasons why they were extended to intelligence investigations. The Fourth Amendment requires that search warrants specify with particularity the place to be searched. This is intended to prevent the accidental or abusive search of an innocent person with, for example, a warrant obtained to search the home of another. As originally applied to electronic surveillance, the particularity requirement meant that law enforcement officers had to specify the particular phone they were intercepting.

Roving wiretap authority is a response to changing technology. Our original electronic surveillance laws stem from a time when phones were fixed in one place and linked to a network by a hard copper wire. Today, when phones can cross state and international boundaries at the speed of flight and where they are disconnected from any physical network, that model is antiquated.

In response to these changes in technology, in 1986 Congress authorized a relaxation of the particularity requirement for the investigation of drug offenses. Under the modified law, the authority to intercept an individual's electronic communication was tied only to the individual who was the suspect of criminal activity (and who was attempting to "thwart" surveillance by, for example, changing phones or locations frequently) rather than to a particular communications device. In 1998, Congress altered the standards somewhat to permit use of a roving wiretap when the target's conduct in changing telephones or facilities had the effect of thwarting the surveillance. Prior to September 11, it was not clear that these authorities could be used to track terrorists, independent of predication to believe a crime was being planned. To clarify the law, and to close the potential gap, section 206 authorized similar techniques for foreign intelligence investigations—an extension that, on its face, seems reasonable.

My colleague agrees generally, but proposes two modifications of existing law. He begins, however, from a premise with which I disagree—that the relaxation of the particularity requirement is constitutionally suspect. That premise influences, I suspect, much of the analysis: but it is, I think, not well founded. To be sure, no court has addressed the constitutionality of section 206, and the Supreme Court has yet to pass on the constitutionality of roving wiretaps generally. But it isn't as if the courts have never addressed roving wiretaps at all—indeed, every appellate court to consider the constitutionality of roving wiretaps has held that they do not violate the particularity requirements of the Constitution, reflecting a contextual understanding that these investigative practices are reasonable.

Reflecting this constitutional hesitancy, the opening essay suggests two modifications to existing requirements—an ascertainment requirement and a heightened identification requirement. Both seem unnecessary and unwise.

The imposition of an ascertainment requirement on law enforcement and intelligence agents would burden their ability to monitor the activities of suspected terrorists and, at the margin, decrease the utility of section 206. Where opponents see the prospect of the interception of innocent conversations, proponents are concerned that during the delay while an ascertainment is being made, or in circumstances where an ascertainment is uncertain, vital terrorism intelligence will be lost. The question then is the balance of risks and benefits. While the balance struck by the ascertainment requirement may make sense in the traditional criminal context, it makes less sense in the context of terrorism investigations.

To begin with, the statute has substantial safeguards against misconduct already—no interception may be authorized unless there is probable cause to believe that the target of the surveillance is a foreign power or an agent of a foreign power. There must also be probable cause to believe that "each of the facilities or places at which the surveillance is directed is being used, or about to be used," by the foreign agent who is the target of the surveillance.

These requirements are subject to both administrative and judicial scrutiny prior to authorization, limiting substantially the chances that a "fishing expedition" of innocents will be initiated. In addition, a minimization requirement mandates the termination of surveillance upon the determination that an intercepted conversation is innocent. Given these protections, there is little that the ascertainment requirement adds to the analysis and much harm it can do in creating hesitancy in our terrorism investigations.

But the ascertainment requirement is wrong for a more fundamental reason: It imposes a narrow law enforcement paradigm on the efforts to combat terrorism. The traditional law enforcement model is highly protective of civil liberty in preference to physical security. The post-September 11 world changes this calculus, principally by changing the costs from a mistake. Whatever the costs of failing to collect information regarding organized crime boss John Gotti might be, they are considerably less than the potentially horrific costs of failing to stop the next Al Qaeda assault. Thus, the theoretical rights-protective construct under which our law enforcement system operates must, of necessity, be modified to meet the new reality. We simply cannot afford a rule that "better 10 terrorists go unscrutinized than that one innocent be mistakenly subject to surveillance." Asserting a direct equivalence between terrorist investigations and the traditional law enforcement construct—which is what the ascertainment requirement does—misses this point altogether.

Consider next the identification requirement. Under the PATRIOT Act, agents may seek authority for an interception even when the identity of the suspect is not known (as long as probable cause exists to believe the person involved was an agent of a foreign power). Imposing a more substantial identification requirement would change that regime. If adopted, it would require agents seeking authority for a wiretap to specify the identity of the target and, if they were unable to do so, to describe with specificity the nature and location of the places where the interception would occur. In other words, in certain circumstances, intelligence agents might be unable to secure a warrant to conduct electronic surveillance because of the indefiniteness of their information.

The proposed modification of section 206, I submit, misses the point. To the extent that it calls for specificity with respect to the precise location or facility where the communication is occurring, it is a non sequitur. Government agents use roving wiretaps only when the location or facility where the communication is occurring is not known with precision—for the simple reason that those under surveillance are attempting to thwart surveillance by constantly changing their location and means of communication. They may have probable cause about a type or class of communications, but lack a particular description of the next "throwaway" cell phone that will be used.

The alternate proposal to require that the individual who is the subject of scrutiny be precisely identified is equally unwise. In a domestic investigation, the identity of the suspect under scrutiny may often be well known, though drug dealers do, of course, use aliases. The problem becomes substantially more acute in the shadowy world of espionage and terrorism, where the identity of the investigative subject is often obscured behind a gauze of deceit.

Terrorists change their identity with frequency and often pose as other, real-world individuals. Often, the only description that the intelligence agency will be able to provide to identify the suspect is an alias (or several aliases). Sometimes the description of the terrorism suspect may be nothing more than a physical description. And, on still other occasions, it may consist only of a pattern of behavior (i.e., the person who regularly uses this series of phones, in this order, every third day). To insist that intelligence and law enforcement agents precisely identify the individual under scrutiny or the facility he will be using is, in effect, to limit the use of roving wiretaps in terrorism investigations.

Finally, it bears noting that there is no practical necessity for the proposed revisions. Though section 206 has been the law of the land for more than three years, there have been no reported instances of abuse of this authority—despite scrutiny by the courts, Congress, and the Department of Justice's Inspector General. Apparently, the Department and the courts are applying the laws in ways that constrain discretion adequately. Whatever else may be said about the PATRIOT Act, even its most ardent critics must admit that they are basing their legislative proposals on the fear of potential abuse rather than reality of actual abuse.

James X. Dempsey

Response

Courts have upheld the constitutionality of roving taps in the criminal context precisely because those roving taps have the guiding standards that are missing from section 206.

The Constitution requires all search warrants (a wiretap order is basically a search warrant) to "particularly describe the place to be searched." Recognizing the crafty mobility of terrorists and other criminals, courts have held that this requirement can be satisfied by describing with particularity either the place (that is, the phone number or Internet account) to be monitored or the person to be monitored. The problem with section 206 of the PATRIOT Act, as modified by the 2002 intelligence authorization act, is that it allows the issuing of roving tap orders without describing either the place or the person. While this leaves roving tap authority for national security cases on shaky ground, it can be clarified without tying the hands of intelligence agents.

The prior essay, by arguing that criminal standards are inapplicable to terrorism investigations, confuses the principles applicable at the trial stage of a criminal case with the much looser rules applicable at the investigative stage. In criminal and intelligence investigations alike, the law allows the government to cast a very broad net. Proponents of fixing the PATRIOT Act's surveillance provisions are not proposing standards suited to criminal trials.

We are saying that bedrock constitutional principles must be followed in both criminal and intelligence investigations, and the particularity requirement is one such bedrock.

Another important protection is the so-called ascertainment requirement. The purpose of roving taps is to follow the bad guy, so unless the bad guy is being followed, the roving tap cannot and should not be activated.

The prior essay presents a false choice between fighting terrorism, on the one hand, and preserving the civil liberties of innocent people on the other. True, we have checks and balances in part to protect the innocent. But we impose limits on government agents also in order to focus their activities and make them more effective. The ascertainment requirement serves to focus government surveillance resources—it ensures that the FBI is not going on a surveillance without reason to believe that the targeted person is using a particular phone or computer. In this way, the ascertainment requirement aids the fight against terrorism.

The prior essay does not really explain why ascertainment would be burdensome. If an officer is required to end surveillance after determining that the wiretap is intercepting the communication of innocent persons, it hardly seems onerous to require the officer to determine that the target is using the communication device before activating the wiretap in the first instance.

Without additional safeguards, section 206 roving tap orders are little different from the "general warrants" that the Fourth Amendment prohibits.

Paul Rosenzweig

The Last Word

There is no false choice between preserving civil liberty and fighting terrorism. To the contrary, the right answer is to seek to maximize both values to the extent it is possible. In that regard, the ascertainment provision championed by the competing essay is one that misses the mark.

First, the ascertainment requirement in criminal law (18 U.S.C. § 2518(12)) applies only to "oral communications" (i.e., those revealed by a hidden microphone) and does not apply to the interception of "wire" or "electronic" communications, like the telephonic conversations subject to interception under section 206. Thus, the ascertainment requirement advanced as a response to the "problem" of roving wiretaps takes a rule used in criminal cases only for oral conversations (like those of Mafia members in an eating club) and applies it to telephonic and electronic communications. But this means that if the ascertainment requirement were adopted, it would be something totally new to electronic interceptions and actually make it more difficult to intercept the telephonic communications of terrorists than of drug dealers—surely not the ideal answer.

Of equal importance, the companion essay does little to demonstrate the necessity of the ascertainment requirement in practical terms. Relying on the robust minimization requirements that continue to exist, the essay posits that ascertainment prior to use is just as easy as minimization once use begins.

But the reality is far different—minimization is based upon knowledge of ongoing conversations, while ascertainment is based upon suppositions regarding future events. It is absolutely predictable that the uncertainty of ascertainment will cause hesitancy in the initiation of an interception. And through the gap created by that hesitancy will flow terrorist communications. Thus, given the probable cause requirements for a section 206 warrant and the minimization protections, the benefits of the ascertainment rule are modest at best, while the costs are likely to be quite real.

Sections 209, 212, and 220.
Access to Wire and Electronic Communications

James X. Dempsey
Orin Kerr

Summary

Mary DeRosa

Sections 209, 212, and 220 adjust certain requirements for access to communications.

Section 209. Previously, seizure of voice-mail stored with a service provider required a court order under the Title III wiretap authorities, which has more rigorous standards than an ordinary criminal search warrant. Stored e-mail, however, required only an ordinary search warrant or in some cases only a subpoena. Section 209 revises 18 U.S.C section 2703 to cover stored voice-mail as well as stored e-mail, thereby eliminating the wiretap order requirement.

Section 212. Electronic communications privacy laws prohibit service providers from voluntarily disclosing, even to the government, most customer communications or records. Section 212 creates an exception to this rule—for both communications and records. It permits providers to disclose this material if they "reasonably believe" that there is "an emergency involving immediate danger of death or physical injury to any person." The exception involving emergency disclosure of the content of communications was made permanent subsequent to the PATRIOT Act by the Home-

31

land Security Act. The exception involving customer records remains subject to the PATRIOT Act sunset provision.

Section 220. Previously, the government could seek a search warrant for service providers' customer communications or records only in the judicial district in which the provider is located. This posed problems for criminal investigators because providers are often located somewhere other than where a crime occurs. Section 220 authorizes the court in the district in which the crime occurred to issue search warrants to be served anywhere in the country. A separate section—section 219, which does not sunset—provides for nationwide service of federal search and arrest warrants in international or domestic terrorism cases.

James X. Dempsey

Why Sections 209, 212, and 220 Should Be Modified

Sections 209, 212, and 220 are not among the most controversial provisions of the PATRIOT Act. The fact that they are subject to the sunset at all, while, for example, the "sneak and peek" authority in section 213 and the national security letter expansions in sections 358 and 505 are not subject to the sunset, is another illustration of how the debate over the sunsets is somewhat misplaced. As with most other sunsetted provisions, there is little call for denying government the access to information provided under sections 209, 212, and 220. Rather, the questions posed by these sections are matters of checks and balances, related to the continuing but uneven effort to rationalize the standards for government access to electronic communications and stored records in the light of ongoing changes in technology.

In that regard, these sections highlight an overarching concern about the way in which amendments to the surveillance laws in recent years, and especially in the PATRIOT Act, have served as a "one-way ratchet" expanding government power without corresponding improvements in the checks and balances applicable to those powers. This has actually been a departure from Congress's traditional approach to electronic surveillance issues. In Title III (1968), in the Electronic Communications Privacy Act of 1986, and even in the controversial Communications Assistance for Law Enforcement Act of 1994, Congress and the Justice Department agreed on the twin goals of ensuring law enforcement authority to intercept communications while also strengthening privacy protection standards, especially in light of changing technology.

This spirit of balance has unfortunately been lost. In recent years, time and again, the Department of Justice has proposed changes in the surveillance laws that reduce judicial oversight or increase executive branch discretion, and Congress has too often enacted them, without ever considering how these changes add up or whether other changes may be needed to increase privacy protections in response to advancements in technology that have made the government's surveillance more intrusive.

In this context, it is easier to see why even some of the minor changes in the PATRIOT Act draw concern, for they are part of a steady stream of uni-directional amendments that are slowly eroding the protections and limits of the electronic privacy laws.

Section 209 permits the seizure of voice-mail messages pursuant to a search warrant or, if the voice-mail has been in storage for a long time, pursuant to a subpoena. Previously, while voice-mail messages stored on an answering machine in one's home could be seized by a search warrant, access to voice-mail messages stored with a service provider had required a Title III order, which offers higher protections. The theory behind section 209 is that stored voice messages should be treated the same as stored data. On some level, this makes the rules technology-neutral, which is usually desirable.

However, the change overlooks the importance of notice under the Fourth Amendment and under Title III, and the absence of notice under the rules applied to stored material held by a service provider. When voice-mail stored on your home answering machine is seized, you are normally provided notice at the time of the search. You can examine the warrant and immediately assert your rights. When e-mail or voice-mail is seized from a service provider pursuant to a warrant, you as the subscriber may never be provided notice unless and until the government introduces the information against you at trial. If you were mistakenly targeted or the government chooses not to use the evidence, you need never be told of the search of your stored communications, so you have little meaningful opportunity to seek redress.

Section 209 removes stored voice-mail from the host of protections afforded under Title III. These extra protections are intended in part to make up for the lack of contemporaneous notice (as well as for the ongoing nature of the intrusion). However, in the case of stored messages (whether e-mail or voice-mail), it is not even necessary from an investigative standpoint to deny contemporaneous notice in the way it is with live interception. Denial of notice is justified in the case of interceptions because the effectiveness of the technique would be destroyed if the target were given contemporaneous notice. In the case of stored e-mail or stored voice messages, the evidence is already created.

A storage revolution is sweeping the field of information and communications technology. Service providers are offering very large quantities of online storage, for e-mail and potentially for voice-mail. Increasingly, technology users are storing information not in their homes or even on portable devices but on networks, under the control of service providers who can be served with compulsory process and never have to tell the subscribers that their privacy has been invaded. New Voice over Internet Protocol (VoIP) services may include the capability to store past voice conversations in a way never available before, further obliterating the distinction between real-time interception and access to stored communications.

Section 209 takes a seemingly small category of information out of the full protection of the Fourth Amendment and moves it under the lowered protections accorded to remotely stored communications and data. But stored voice-mail is the tip of an iceberg. Rather than allowing growing amounts of personal information to fall outside the traditional protections of the Fourth Amendment, it is time to revisit the rules for networked storage (whether of voice or data) and bring them more in line with traditional Fourth Amendment principles, by requiring contemporaneous notice as the norm and covering both newer records and older records (again, whether voice or data) under the same probable cause standard. That would be truly technology-neutral and would have the advantage of not allowing technology advances to erode privacy protections.

Section 212 permits service providers to voluntarily disclose the contents of communications and transactional information without compulsory process in emergency situations. Section 212 represents another in a steadily growing series of exceptions to the protections of the electronic communications privacy laws. (The computer trespasser provision of section 217 is another example.) Section 212 and similar provisions essentially allow "off the books surveillance"—they define certain interceptions not to be interceptions, and certain disclosures not to be disclosures. Once an access to communications or data is excluded from the coverage of the surveillance laws, not only is it not subject to prior judicial approval, but there are no time limits on the period covered by the surveillance or disclosure, no minimization requirement, no report back to a judge, no notice to the persons who are surveilled unless and until the government introduces the evidence against them in a criminal trial, no statutory suppression rule, and no reports to Congress and the public.

Emergency exceptions are of course reasonable. And the standard in section 212 is not facially objectionable "if the provider reasonably believes that an emergency involving immediate danger of death or physical injury to any person requires [or justifies] disclosure of the information." It should be recognized, however, that the information about the emergency will often come from a government agent. Rather than going to a judge and getting a warrant, section 212 permits a government agent to go to a service provider, say there is an emergency, and if the service provider reasonably believes there is (even if the government agent was exaggerating), the service provider can disclose the records with no liability and no notice to the subscriber. Surely, this is an invitation to cutting corners, if not more cynical forms of abuse. Notice also how placing the reasonable belief on the part of the service provider diffuses responsibility: the stored records provisions to which this exception was added has no suppression rule for evidence improperly obtained, and it does not appear that the civil action and administrative discipline provisions of 18 U.S.C. section 2707 would apply to agents who even intentionally mislead a service provider about the existence of an emergency.

In an age when warrants can be obtained by telephone or fax and presumably even by e-mail, *see* Federal Rule of Criminal Procedure 41(d)(3), and when every court should have a duty judge available by cell phone or Blackberry 24 hours a day, it is not really so clear that emergency exceptions to judicial oversight are necessary. But even if they are, they should not fall entirely outside a system of checks and balances.

Checks and balances should be added to section 212. Under the emergency exceptions of both Title III and FISA, after an emergency interception has begun, there must still be an application to a judge, and the information obtained under the assertion of emergency must be discarded if authority to intercept is subsequently denied, and under Title III the application, whether granted or denied, becomes subject to notice requirements. Similar principles could be applied to the emergency authority of section 212: it could be revised to require after-the-fact review by a judge, and if the judge does not find that the disclosure would otherwise have been justified, the information could be suppressed. At the least, the person whose privacy has been invaded should be notified that his information has been disclosed to the government. An additional or alternative protection would be to make it illegal for a government official to intentionally or recklessly mislead a service provider as to the existence of an emergency. Coupled with notice, this could provide a reasonable remedy to persons whose privacy was needlessly invaded.

Other parts of section 212 are non-controversial: it rearranged sections 2702 and 2703 of title 18 to make them more logical and clarified that service providers have the statutory authority to disclose non-content records to protect their rights and property.

Note: The change made by section 212 covering emergency disclosures of the content of communications was repealed by the act creating the Homeland Security Department and replaced with a new and permanent emergency disclosure provision. The comments made above about checks and balances pertain to the new language as well.

Section 220 amended 18 U.S.C. section 2703 to allow judges to issue search warrants for electronic evidence that can be executed outside of the district in which the issuing court is located. In a world where the center of an investigation may be in one state but the target's ISP has its servers in another state, this makes obvious sense. However, as the Electronic Privacy Information Center has noted, section 220 removes "an important legal safeguard by making it more difficult for a distant service provider to appear before the issuing court and object to legal or procedural defects. Indeed, it has become increasingly common for service providers to seek clarification from issuing courts when, in the face of rapidly evolving technological changes, many issues involving the privacy rights of their subscribers require careful judicial consideration. The burden would be particularly acute for smaller providers." One solution to this problem is to allow a warrant to be challenged not only in the district in which it was issued but also in the district in which it is served. While the issuing judge may have a better sense of the factual basis for the order, a judge in the district in which the order is served may be in a better position to interpret or redefine the scope of the order in light of issues concerning the system of the service provider on whom the order is served. Even aside from section 220, whether search warrants for electronic evidence are issued for evidence inside or outside their jurisdictions, judges should question applicants to be sure that the warrant is narrowly drawn. Judges should use extra care in understanding what information is being sought, whether it will be copied or originals will be seized (interfering with ongoing business), and whether it is possible to disclose just certain fields or just records from a certain pertinent time frame. These are analogous to questions that judges have the authority to consider in the case of physical searches, but judges need to understand computer systems in order to fully enforce the specificity requirement of the Fourth Amendment in the digital context. Judges should look more carefully at the return of service. While notice under 18 U.S. C. section 2705(b) can be prohibited, judges should be hesitant to deny notice to the person to whom the records pertain, since the subscriber is really in the best position to raise legitimate concerns. This is just another way in which judges faced with the authorities of the PATRIOT Act can assert closer scrutiny and place conditions on the exercise of PATRIOT authorities without denying the government access to the information needed.

Orin Kerr

Reply

Sections 209, 212, and 220 match statutory surveillance laws to the traditional protections of the Fourth Amendment. These sections try to ensure that on-line investigations are regulated by the same principles that regulate investigations off-line under the Fourth Amendment. This is a laudable and generally uncontroversial goal, and it should be unsurprising that these sections have drawn little controversy. Congress should retain them.

To understand these sections of the PATRIOT Act, it helps to begin by understanding why Congress regulates Internet privacy instead of the courts and the Fourth Amendment. Sections 209, 212, and 220 exist because the Fourth Amendment extends little if any privacy protection to Internet communications. The Fourth Amendment does a very good job regulating traditional criminal investigations, in which the police enter private homes and retrieve evidence. Fourth Amendment rules regulate when the police can search the home and what property they can seize once there. The basic rule is that a probable cause warrant is required to enter a home and retrieve evidence unless an exception such as exigent circumstances applies.

When we switch from traditional investigations to Internet crime cases, however, the Fourth Amendment suddenly offers little protection. Evidence such as e-mail is now stored with third-party Internet service providers, and the police generally try to obtain the information directly from those service providers. But the Fourth Amendment generally offers no protection to information disclosed to third parties, and gives those third parties unlimited power to search through documents in their possession and disclose the results to law enforcement. Although the constitutional doctrine in this area is not well-developed, the cases suggest that the Fourth Amendment may offer little or even no protection to Internet users.

The gap in constitutional protection triggers an obvious need for congressional regulation. Congress must step in to protect what the Constitution does not. Fortunately, Congress acted at a very early stage to confer this protection: it enacted a comprehensive statute in 1986 called the Electronic Communications Privacy Act (ECPA). ECPA erected a complicated statutory framework that generates the equivalent of off-line Fourth Amendment protections on-line by statute. The statute restricts the power of investigators to compel evidence from ISPs and places limits on the ability of ISPs to voluntarily disclose information about their subscribers. The basic goal of the statute is to create Fourth Amendment–like protections for Internet communications. Sections 209, 212, and 220 are all amendments to ECPA.

These amendments are necessary because while ECPA was a remarkable achievement for its day, it had a number of quirks and gaps in need of correction. For example, Congress forgot to include an "exigent circumstances" exception for records. The Fourth Amendment contains a common-sense exception to the warrant requirement permitting officers to search and seize if exigent circumstances such as an emergency require immediate action and obtaining a warrant is impractical. ECPA had no such exception for records, however. If an exigency occurred, the police simply were out of luck: the police could not compel ISPs to act without a warrant, and ISPs were also forbidden to disclose information voluntarily in response to the exigency. In a stark departure from well-established Fourth Amendment law, exigent circumstances became irrelevant.

ECPA also had adopted a rather strange rule to regulate voice-mail stored with service providers. ECPA required the police to obtain a super-warrant Title III wiretapping order to compel unopened voice-mail, but offered zero privacy protection for opened voice-mail. Requiring a Title III super warrant effectively placed unopened voice-mail off-limits for the police, treating voice-mail as more private than personal diaries and bedrooms. Under ECPA, if the government knew that there was one copy of an unopened private message in a person's bedroom and another copy on their remotely stored voice-mail, it was illegal for the FBI to simply obtain the voice-mail; the law actually compelled the police to invade the home and rifle through peoples' bedrooms so as not to disturb the more private voice-mail. Similarly, the law flatly barred state and local police from obtaining access to voice-mail except in extremely rare situations. At the same time, ECPA left already-accessed voice-mail completely unregulated by any statutory privacy law. This regulatory approach made little sense.

Finally, ECPA introduced needless delay in investigations by changing the traditional rule that federal investigators can obtain orders to compel information in one district and serve them on third parties in other districts. For example, a federal grand jury subpoena can be obtained in one district and served on a company in another district via mail or fax. In contrast, ECPA required law enforcement either to travel around the country to wherever ISP was located or else get local assistance in order to get a search warrant to compel an ISP to disclose information. The order had to be obtained in the district where the ISP was physically located. If a

New York–based FBI agent needed to compel a California-based ISP to disclose evidence about a New York–based defendant, he needed to travel to California and apply for a warrant there (or else get help from an agent in California who otherwise had no role in the investigation). Once again, this deviation from the traditional rules made little sense.

Sections 209, 212, and 220 cure these three defects in ECPA. Section 212 adds a narrow exigent circumstances exception to ECPA. It permits a service provider to volunteer information to law enforcement if the provider has a reasonable belief that an emergency involving immediate danger of death or serious physical bodily injury to a person requires immediate disclosure. This narrow exception is considerably more privacy-protective than the Fourth Amendment's broad exigent circumstances exception, but reflects a similar effort to balance privacy with competing needs of crime victims. Section 209 corrects ECPA's strange treatment of voice-mail by protecting voice-mail just like other stored content files such as e-mail. The change simultaneously raises the protection for opened voice-mail and extends the traditional Fourth Amendment search warrant protection for unopened voice-mail. Section 220 permits investigators to obtain warrants to compel ISPs to disclose information in the district where they are conducting the investigation just as they would any other order. Investigators no longer need to travel or obtain the assistance of others in faraway districts to obtain court orders. In all three cases, the PATRIOT Act attempts to bring the statutory surveillance law into alignment with the Fourth Amendment.

For the most part, Jim Dempsey's proposals for reform would impose greater privacy restrictions for on-line investigations than equivalent off-line investigations. For example, Dempsey would require a court order to be obtained following an exigent circumstances disclosure, whereas the Fourth Amendment has no such requirement. He would also allow recipients of orders to compel to challenge those orders within the recipient's district rather than in the district where it was issued, instead of retaining the traditional rule that any challenge (itself an extremely rare event) must be filed in the issuing district.

Finally, Dempsey would require customers whose records were disclosed pursuant to an order to compel to receive notice of the disclosure, whereas the Fourth Amendment has no such requirement. While Dempsey suggests that notice is needed to match Fourth Amendment rules, I think his analogy is somewhat flawed. To be sure, the Fourth Amendment normally does require notice to a property owner when the police execute a warrant at a home. However, this notice does not permit the homeowner to challenge the warrant before it is executed, and does not extend to others whose property is located at the place to be searched. According to the Supreme Court, the notice requirement exists so the homeowner knows that the police officers knocking at the door are acting pursuant to proper legal authority and are not rogue officers. Current law appears to satisfy this policy concern by providing notice to the ISP.

This does not mean I necessarily disagree with Dempsey's proposals. I am interested in hearing more about some of them, and less enthusiastic about others. But I see Dempsey's proposals as parallel to the debate over sections 209, 212, and 220, rather than as a direct challenge to those sections. All three provisions are balanced and appropriate efforts to match statutory laws to the Fourth Amendment. Whatever other proposals Congress wishes to consider beyond them, it should begin by reaffirming these uncontroversial sections of the PATRIOT Act.

James X. Dempsey

Response

A crucial challenge posed by new technologies is how to extend to them privacy protections equivalent to those afforded by the Fourth Amendment. A one-to-one extension is difficult, especially since, about 30 years ago, the Supreme Court held that the

Constitution affords no privacy protection to personal information disclosed to "third parties." Under this theory, the government can get your financial records from your bank and your prescription drug records from your pharmacy merely by asking the third party to disclose them, with no notice to you and no opportunity for you to object.

Even 30 years ago, this seemed at odds with people's reasonable expectations. Today, in the digital age, this theory, unless Congress acts, would leave unprotected the vast quantities of information about almost every aspect of your life that are recorded with businesses. The transition to Web-based services and the availability of huge volumes of on-line storage mean that e-mails, calendars, travel itineraries, photos, documents, and even drafts never meant to be read by anyone are stored outside the protections of the Constitution. Professor Kerr agrees that unless the Supreme Court revisits its "third-party records" doctrine, Congress has to respond, as it did in the Electronic Communications Privacy Act of 1986. Professor Kerr also agrees that some of the protections of that statute are no longer adequate, given the continuing evolution of the networked society. Our dispute is over what further changes are necessary to respond to the flow of information out of the home and onto the Internet.

In my view, one of the most important of the "traditional" Fourth Amendment protections is notice when the government is seeking information about you. (One of the few exceptions would be wiretapping, where the effectiveness of the technique would be obviated if prior or contemporaneous notice were given.) Under ECPA, and under sections 209, 212, and 220 of the PATRIOT Act, the government can get your records from a third party without telling you. Without transparency, the government is much more likely to ask for a lot, and the business receiving the order is not likely to want to spend its money defending your privacy.

Section 212 allows the government to tell an ISP that there is an emergency, and the ISP can then disclose your e-mail without even a subpoena, let alone a warrant, and never tell you so that you never have an opportunity to challenge the disclosure. Traditionally, when records were stored locally, even if there was an emergency justifying an exception to the warrant requirement, you would normally know of the search of your home or office. At the least, under 212, there should be after-the-fact notice to the person whose e-mail has been disclosed and some opportunity to judge whether the government fairly represented the existence of an emergency.

Section 209 allows the government to use a mere subpoena to get voicemail you have listened to but continue to store with the phone company's voicemail service, again without notice. Notice and an opportunity to object in non-emergency situations would protect against abuse of practices now shrouded in secret.

Secrecy is not necessary in these situations to ensure the success of the investigation: the information is stored with a third party, outside your control, so the government will get it even if it gives you notice.

Orin Kerr

Common Ground, But a Few Questions

Jim Dempsey and I agree about a great deal here: I think our area of disagreement is a relatively minor one about means, not a fundamental one about ends.

My own view is that the problems Dempsey identifies can be best addressed in two ways: first, by adding a statutory suppression remedy to the Internet surveillance laws; and second, by bolstering some of the privacy protections for accessed communications under the Stored Communications Act. I have written law review articles urging Congress to make both changes: *Lifting the 'Fog' of Internet Surveillance: How a Suppression Remedy Would Change Computer Crime Law,* 54 HASTINGS LAW JOURNAL 805-45 (2003) (arguing in favor of a suppression remedy), and *A User's Guide to the Stored Communications Act, and a Legislator's Guide to Amending It,* 72 GEORGE WASHINGTON LAW REVIEW 1208-43

(2004) (arguing both for a suppression remedy and for bolstered protection for opened e-mail and voice-mail). Both articles are available on Westlaw and LEXIS, and can be downloaded for free at www.patriotdebates.com.

Jim Dempsey's concerns about notice are serious ones that merit substantial attention. They raise an interesting and difficult question: what right should a person have to know that the government has obtained information about him or her, either before or after that information has been obtained? The traditional rule in criminal investigations is that notice need not be given. For example, a suspect has no right to know when government investigators subpoena a suspect's phone records, look up their criminal records, open an undercover investigation, talk to the suspect's neighbors, or interview eyewitnesses to the crime. The only major exception is that residents have a right to know when the government has executed a search warrant in that person's home: although there is no absolute right to notice, the usual rule is that the police must leave notice that the search occurred. Under current law, Internet users also have a narrow right to notice when the government seeks to obtain content records from an ISP with less than probable cause.

Should this narrow right be expanded to include other kinds of government access to information stored by Internet service providers? Perhaps, perhaps not. The traditional rule against notice reflects a legitimate government interest: notice tips off the suspect as to the details of the investigation, and that notice can thwart the investigation. Notice can also add a paperwork requirement that ranges from minimal to substantial. At the same time, notice can provide a target with the information needed to challenge the government's procedure. My instinct is that the interest served by the notice requirement is best met instead by a statutory suppression remedy. A suppression remedy would require notice after criminal charges are brought and permit defendants to challenge the government's procedure at that point. But if Congress does not wish to add a suppression remedy, greater notice requirements at the time of government access to information should be considered.

Section 214.
Pen Register and Trap and Trace Authority Under FISA

Section 215.
Access to Business Records Under FISA (Libraries Provision)

Andrew C. McCarthy
Peter P. Swire

Summary

Mary DeRosa

Section 215 revises substantially the authority under FISA for seizure of business records, including third-party records of individuals' transactions and activities. Previously, FISA section 501 permitted the FBI to apply to the Foreign Intelligence Surveillance Court (FISC) for an order to seize business records of hotels, motels, car and truck rental agencies, and storage rental facilities. Section 215 broadens that authority by eliminating any limitation on the types of businesses or entities whose records may be seized. In addition, the section expands the scope of the items that the FBI may obtain using this authority from "records" to "any tangible things (including books, records, papers, documents, and other items)." The recipient of the order may not disclose the fact that the FBI has sought or obtained records.

Section 215 also eases the requirements for obtaining an order to seize business records. Previously, FISA required the FBI to present

47

the FISC "specific articulable facts giving reason to believe" that the subject of an investigation was a "foreign power or the agent of a foreign power." After section 215, the government is required only to assert that the records or things are sought for a foreign intelligence investigation or to protect against international terrorism or clandestine intelligence activities, although the investigation of a United States person may not be "solely upon the basis of activities protected by the first amendment to the Constitution." There is no requirement for an evidentiary or factual showing and the judge has little discretion in reviewing an application. If the judge finds that "the application meets the requirements" of the section, he or she must issue an order as requested "or as modified."

Section 214 makes similar changes to procedures for obtaining pen register or trap and trace orders under FISA. "Pen registers" and "trap and trace" devices record information about the recipient and source, respectively, of a communication. They do not intercept the contents of communications. Previously, FISA section 402 required the government to certify to the FISC that there was reason to believe a line monitored by one of these devices would be used by an individual or a foreign power engaged in international terrorism or spying that violates U.S. criminal laws. After section 214, there is no such certification required. Instead, the certification requirements are similar to those described above for business records.

Section 216, which does not sunset, changed the definitions of "pen register" and "trap and trace" to clarify that they apply to e-mail and Internet, as well as telephone communications.

Andrew C. McCarthy

Why Sections 214 and 215 Should Be Retained

Sections 214 and 215 of the PATRIOT Act expanded the government's authority under the Foreign Intelligence Surveillance Act (50 U.S.C. § 1801 et seq. (2000 ed.)) to, respectively, conduct pen register/trap-and-trace surveillance and compel production of business records. The lion's share of this discussion will focus on section 215.

None of the PATRIOT Act's enhancements of government's investigative arsenal has been more assiduously libeled than section 215. Indeed, in the public mind it has become the "library records" provision, notwithstanding that libraries are nowhere mentioned. While there are points of legitimate concern, most of the controversy is a tempest in a teapot. Section 215 is a good law. It merits being made permanent, albeit with some tailoring to provide expressly for the now-implicit ability of production-order recipients to seek judicial narrowing. Beyond that, altering this provision out of overwrought suspicions about potential abuse would likely, and perversely, result only in greater potential abuse.

Section 215 modified FISA in two ways. The first relates to what information may be compelled. Formerly, this was restricted to travel, lodging, and storage records. Section 215 broadens the scope to include not merely such business records but "any tangible things (including books, records, papers, documents, and other items)."

This is not nearly as dramatic as it appears. For decades, Rule 17 (c), Fed. R. Crim. P., has authorized compulsory production of "any books, papers, documents, data, or other objects" to criminal investigators by mere subpoena. Given the incontestable breadth of the federal criminal statutes implicated by terrorism and espionage, coupled with the broad license grand juries have to conduct investigations, there is no item now obtainable by section 215 that could not already be compelled by simple subpoena (and thus made accessible to intelligence agents, who are now permitted to share grand jury information).

Why such extensive access with virtually no court supervision? Because the items at issue here are primarily activity records voluntarily left in the hands of third parties. As the Supreme Court has long held, such items simply do not involve legitimate expectations of privacy. *See, e.g., Smith v. Maryland*, 442 U.S. 735, 744 (1979). This renders them categorically different from the private information at issue in the context of search warrants or eavesdropping, in which the court is properly imposed as a bulwark, requiring a demonstration of cause before government may pierce established constitutional safeguards.

Thus, while the PATRIOT Act plainly expanded FISA powers, the reality is that prior law governing national security investigations was unnecessarily stingy, especially in contrast to rules that empower criminal agents probing far less serious matters, like gambling. Such incongruities are intolerable in the post-9/11 world, where public safety is critically dependent on intelligence.

Here, one must address the theater over library records, risibly evoking visions of DOJ Thought Police monitoring, and thus chilling, the reading preferences of Americans. First, as demonstrated above, government has long had the authority to compel reading records by subpoena; yet there is no empirical indication of systematic prying into private choices—else we'd surely have heard from the robustly organized librarians. Second, leaving aside that agents (who are also Americans) generally lack voyeuristic interest in the public's reading and viewing habits, investigations in the Information Age are simply too demanding for such shenanigans. Naturally, one could never eliminate the occasional rogue, no matter what precautions were in place; but in the 21st century, voluminous information streams and finite resources leave no time for this sort of malfeasance. Third, and most significant, it does not diminish our society's high regard for personal liberty to observe that an a priori ban on investigative access to reading records would be both unprecedented and dangerous.

In point of fact, literature evidence was a staple of terrorism prosecutions throughout the 1990s. Terrorists read bomb manuals and often leave fingerprints on pages spelling out explosive recipes that match the forensics of particular bombings (like the 1993 attack on the World Trade Center). Possession of jihadist writings is also relevant in the cases of accused terrorists who, having pled not guilty, put the government to its burden of proving knowledge and intent. Of course we don't want FBI agents snooping around libraries for no good reason; but do we really want terrorists immunized from the properly prejudicial effects of probative evidence—evidence that has proven key to past convictions? Americans value many species of privacy but sensibly allow them to be overcome when relevant evidence of even minor crime is at stake. It would be extremely unwise to create hurdles for library evidence that don't exist for items stored in a person's own bedroom, or to create impediments in national security cases that don't exist in, say, routine drug investigations.

The second major change wrought by section 215 involves the showing required before a FISA production order is issued. Previously, agents were called on to provide "specific and articulable facts giving reason to believe that" the records pertained to an agent of a foreign power. Now, the order must issue upon the government's representation that it seeks to obtain intelligence concerning non-U.S. persons, or to protect against international terrorism or espionage.

Practically speaking, this change is, again, less dramatic than appears on the surface. Consider the contrast: in criminal investigations, there is no court supervision at all over government's issuance of subpoenas. Section 215, moreover, expressly prohibits FISA investigations based "solely on . . . activities protected by the First Amendment"; criminal probes carry no such protection.

Concededly, however, defenders of section 215, rather than explaining why court supervision of investigations would be improper, tend counterproductively to stress the court-order requirement. Illustrative is the Justice Department's highlighting that "Section 215 requires FBI agents to get a court order." (See "Dispelling the Myths" (emphasis in original).) Though accurate, this assertion may inadvertently imply searching judicial review. In fact, section 215 provides no such thing: if the government makes the prescribed representations, the FISA court is without discretion to deny the order. This is precisely as it should be, but people who have assumed a degree of judicial scrutiny understandably become alarmed upon learning it is a false assumption.

Yes, section 215's judicial exercise is ministerial, but that does not make it unique or inconsequential. It is analogous to familiar pen register law, under which a judge must issue the authorization upon the request of criminal investigators, with no demonstration of cause. Why? Because our system is premised on separation of powers. Investigation is an executive function. The judicial role is not to supervise the executive but to protect U.S. persons against improper invasions of legitimate expectations of privacy. People do not have such expectations regarding the phone numbers they dial, thus a ministerial judicial role is appropriate: the order issues on the court's power, but it is not the judiciary's place to question bona fides of a co-equal branch carrying out its own constitutional function.

In matters of national security more than any other investigative realm, it is crucial to remain mindful of the court's institutional competence. The judiciary's limited role is to protect established constitutional interests, not create new ones as a means to micromanage investigations. When neither U.S. persons nor legitimate expectations of privacy are involved, as is generally the case with section 215, a court has no cause to demand an explanation of the basis for the FBI's application.

So why require going to the court at all? Because, as is the case with grand jury subpoenas (which are court orders though issued without court supervision), it is appropriate that the directive to comply comes from the judicial power. Moreover, section 215 prudently charges Congress with the responsibility of ensuring that the executive branch is not abusing its authority. By requiring the FBI to make solemn representations to the court, and mandating that the Attorney General report semiannually on this provision's implementation, section 215 provides suitable metrics for oversight and, if necessary, reform.

Finally, the formerly mandated articulation hinders proper investigations. Emblematic is the pre-9/11 Zacharias Moussaoui scenario. There are times when the FBI will have solid reason to suspect that a person is a terrorist operative (as Moussaoui's flight school behavior aroused suspicion), but not yet have developed enough evidence to tie the suspect to a particular foreign power (such as Al Qaeda). In such a case, given that the Fourth Amendment poses no obstacle to the FBI's access to third-party records, the safety of Americans assuredly should not be imperiled for the benefit of a non-U.S. person by burdening investigators with a legally unnecessary showing that it will not be possible for them to meet.

Section 215 should be amended to clarify that order recipients may move the FISA court to quash or narrow production. This remedy is available in the analogous context of grand jury subpoenas, the Justice Department has appropriately taken the position that it is implicit in section 215, and it will incentivize investigators to minimize their applications responsibly.

Further modification would be legally unnecessary, as well as unwise policy. Raising the access bar would simply encourage government to proceed by grand jury subpoena or national security letter—guaranteeing less judicial participation, more difficult congressional oversight, and the inefficiency of quash litigation in district courts throughout the country, rather than in the FISA court (a salient reason for whose creation was to develop specialized expertise in the sensitive issues unique to intelligence investigations).

In light of its relatedness to section 215, section 214 need not detain us long. This provision sensibly extends the pen register/ trap-and-trace device procedures already available for telephone communications to the newer technologies of e-mail and Internet. Importantly, this does not permit government to invade the content of communications; all that is at stake here is routing and addressing information.

Prior FISA law required government to certify that the monitored communications would likely be those either of an international terrorist or spy involved in a violation of U.S. criminal law, or of an agent of a foreign power involved in terrorism or espionage. This was an unnecessary and imprudently high hurdle. The Supreme Court, as noted above, has long held that pen registers do not implicate any Fourth Amendment interests—they are not searches, they do not invade legitimate expectations of privacy, and there is no constitutional reason to require investigators to seek court authorization for them at all.

Consequently, section 214's modification of prior law is both modest and eminently reasonable. Agents are still required to obtain a court order before installing a pen register. In addition, they are still required to make a solemn representation to the court; now, however, that is limited to certifying that the information sought would be relevant to an investigation to protect against international terrorism or clandestine intelligence activities. Though less extensive than before, this still easily passes constitutional muster. It is also comfortably analogous to criminal practice, where investigators must be granted pen register authority upon merely certifying that "the information likely to be obtained is relevant to an ongoing criminal investigation[.]" (18 U.S.C. § 3122 (b)(2)). And, as was the case with section 215, section 214 may not be employed to conduct an investigation based solely on activities protected by the First Amendment—a safeguard that does not exist in criminal investigations.

Section 214 should neither be modified nor permitted to sunset.

Peter P. Swire

Reply

Andrew McCarthy has presented a defense of sections 214 and 215 of the PATRIOT Act essentially as drafted, and stated that they should be renewed permanently rather than being allowed to sunset at the end of 2005. Mr. McCarthy gives a clear and articulate statement of positions that the U.S. Department of Justice has presented on these issues. In this response, I explain reasons for considerably greater skepticism toward the current section 215, especially with respect to the so-called "gag rule" provision that Mr. McCarthy does not discuss. I also explain, much more briefly, some concerns with the current section 214. My discussion here builds on my study on "The System of Foreign Intelligence Surveillance Law," published in the *George Washington Law Review* and available in the publications section of my Web site at www.peterswire. net. It also builds on my experience chairing a White House Working Group in 2000 on how to update wiretap and surveillance laws for the Internet age.

The Much Broader Scope of Records Searches Under Section 215

Section 215 of the PATRIOT Act expanded the sweep of Foreign Intelligence Surveillance Act (FISA) orders to compel production of business records and other tangible objects. The original FISA had focused on electronic surveillance and had not created a FISA mechanism for the government to get business records. After the Oklahoma City and first World Trade Center bombings, Congress authorized the use of FISA orders for travel records only.

Section 215 contained two statutory changes that greatly expanded this power. First, the type of records subject to the order went far beyond travel records. Now the search can extend to "any tangible things (including books, records, papers, documents, and other items) . . . ." By its terms, the statute apparently would allow a FISA order to trump other laws that usually govern the release of records, including for medical records and other categories of records that are generally subject to privacy protections.

Second, the legal standard changed for obtaining the order. Previously, the application had to show "specific and articulable facts giving reason to believe that the person to whom the records pertain is a foreign power or an agent of a foreign power." This standard, although less than probable cause, is relatively strict. The PATRIOT Act eliminated the need for any particularized showing. The application need merely "specify that the records concerned are sought for an authorized investigation . . . to protect against international terrorism or clandestine intelligence activities." What counts as an authorized investigation is within the discretion of the executive branch.

Under this change in the text, FISA orders can now apply to anyone, not only the target of the investigation. Previously, the records or other objects sought had to concern either a foreign power or the agent of a foreign power. Now, the FISA order can require production of records about persons who have nothing to do with a foreign power. The only weak restraints include the need for "an authorized investigation" and the requirement that surveillance of U.S. persons not be based solely upon First Amendment activities. This is a significant change, permitting seizure of records of persons who are not the target of an investigation and not an agent of a foreign power. Similarly, by permitting the order to cover records of all persons, the literal terms of section 215 would permit an entire database to be the subject of a FISA order. As long as there is "an authorized investigation," the statute does not set any limits on the type or number of records subject to the FISA order.

Mr. McCarthy makes two principal arguments to support the expansion. First, he explains how the government has similarly broad powers to get records for criminal investigations. One crucial limit applies, however, to criminal investigations but not to section 215 searches—showing that a crime has been, is being, or will be committed. In addition, as discussed further below, section 215 contains what is often called a "gag rule"—"No person shall disclose to any other person (other than those persons necessary to produce the tangible things under this section) that the Federal Bureau of Investigation has sought or obtained tangible things under this section." No similar rule applies to business records produced in the course of a criminal investigation.

Mr. McCarthy's other key argument is that the Supreme Court has found no Fourth Amendment "reasonable expectation of privacy" in records about an individual held by third parties. He describes the records as "voluntarily left in the hands of third parties" such as banks, hospitals, schools, and other record holders, and thus the records should be readily available to the government with far less than a probable cause order. The problem with this constitutional argument—an argument repeatedly made by the Department of Justice—is that it mistakenly asserts that something that is constitutional is also desirable policy. To see this mistake, consider that a 90 percent income tax is almost certainly constitutional, but few people think it therefore would be a wise policy. Especially for sensitive records held by libraries, hospitals, and others, better policy is to have significant oversight by the courts.

A short discussion is necessary on the topic of searches of library records. Mr. McCarthy complains that the "theater" of that debate has been "risibly evoking visions of DOJ Thought Police monitoring." In my view, the debate about access to library records has been important as a symbol of possible overreaching in government surveillance, much as the PATRIOT Act itself has become a symbol of that concern. The debate over library records, moreover, goes to one important reason why we should be concerned about possible government overreaching. The Foreign Intelligence Surveillance Act was passed in 1978 in the wake of Watergate and revelations about systematic surveillance of journalists and of political opponents of the government. Standard First Amendment jurisprudence recognizes the chilling effect on expression and political activity that can result from such surveillance. The debate over library records, then, provides an important way to articulate what is at risk if surveillance expands too far.

In response to public concern about use of section 215 to gather library records, Attorney General Ashcroft reported in September 2003 that the section had never been used since passage of the PATRIOT Act for library or any other records. This lack of usage is reassuring because it shows that the Justice Department has not been using the new power for routine surveillance of library and other sensitive records. The lack of usage also supports the position that the Justice Department has not made the case for renewing section 215 when the sunset expires. There are existing procedures for gathering records without using the extraordinary scope of section 215. Absent some new showing by the Justice Department of the specific circumstances where section 215 is needed, the provision should be allowed to sunset.

If the decision is made to keep some form of section 215, however, then there are various reforms that would cabin some of the most disturbing aspects. For instance, there could be a specific carve-out from section 215 for library records. There could be deference to the medical, financial, and other privacy laws on the books, so that the specific statutes would govern categories of records rather than using the lower standard of section 215. Next, the standard could return to the "specific and articulable facts" standard that existed before 2001, rather than leaving unchecked access to records that simply are part of an investigation. Perhaps most compellingly (and suggested also by Mr. McCarthy), there should be a procedure for record holders to claim that a request is unduly overbroad and burdensome. The Foreign Intelligence Surveillance Court (or federal district court) could provide the same oversight of overbroad and burdensome requests as exists currently for requests in criminal investigations.

The Unjustified Expansion of the "Gag Rule"

An especially troubling aspect of section 215 (and the expanded use of so-called "National Security Letters" under section 505 of the PATRIOT Act) is the provision that makes it illegal for individuals or organizations to reveal that they have been asked by the government to provide documents or other tangible objects. The law makes it criminal for a librarian or any other person even to say that there has been a FISA request, without saying more about the nature of the request or the name of the target. This "gag rule" is an unjustified expansion of a special rule for wiretaps and is contrary to the rules that have historically applied to government requests for records.

There has long been a specialized rule for wiretaps, under both Title III and FISA, that the telephone company and others who implement the wiretap are required to keep the wiretap secret while it is in operation. The need for secrecy flows from the special nature of wiretaps—they don't work nearly as well when the target knows someone is listening. By contrast, a records search (such as under section 215) ordinarily secures the available information for the investigator. Unlike the initiation of the wiretap, the search is complete once the records are produced.

The secrecy requirement for those implementing the wiretap is a special case, entirely different from the legal rules that apply to ordinary government investigations. Suppose that a landlord is interviewed by police about the whereabouts of a tenant or a company is asked for records about its sales to a particular individual. The American approach in such instances is that the landlord or the company is permitted to talk about the investigation with the press or other persons. This ability to speak to the press or others is an important First Amendment right. Under the "gag rule" approach, that right is taken away and individuals subject to excessive searches must risk criminal sanctions even to report overreaching or abuses of government authority.

The general American approach also places key limits on what a landlord or company may say. If a landlord tips off a tenant that the police are trying to catch the tenant, then the landlord is subject to punishment under obstruction of justice, conspiracy, or similar statutes. This kind of targeted criminal sanction permits citizens to keep watch on possible overreaching by the government, while also empowering the government to punish those who assist in criminal activity.

The furor about FISA access to library and other records is based in part on the recognition that this sort of broad search power could expand over time into a routine practice of intrusive domestic surveillance. The combination of this essentially unlimited search power with the "gag rule" means that the most basic check against abuse—publicity—is removed. Similar gag rules have recently spread into other statutes.

What to do about the gag rule? Quite possibly, it simply is not needed. Tips to suspects can be handled under conspiracy and other existing law. If some sort of gag rule is kept for records searches (for fear of tipping off terrorists), then the suppression of speech should be minimized by easily implemented rules. One approach would be to say that the gag order lasts for six months, with the order renewable if the FISC agrees. Another approach is to say that the fact of a search can be announced, but not the name of the suspect. More generally, the FISC judges can use their Article III experience to exercise the same oversight over the gag rule that they do over criminal investigations. Procedures can be added to FISA so that the FISC can keep information secret where appropriate, but with presumptions that the nature of the search can be made public over time, consistent with free speech and accountability of government.

The current gag rule for records was never the subject of hearings or public debate. It is the most objectionable part of section 215.

Section 214

The standard for getting a FISA pen register or trap-and-trace order was simplified in the PATRIOT Act. Previously, these orders could be issued only if there was reason to believe that the telephone line subject to the order had been or was about to be used in communications involving international terrorism or an agent of a foreign power. That requirement was dropped in the PATRIOT Act, with the standard becoming essentially the same as for domestic orders. In 2000, the House Judiciary Committee voted overwhelmingly to raise the standard for a pen register order from "any authorized investigation" to "specific and articulable facts." The issue for both criminal and FISA pen register orders is whether the Committee got it right at that time—whether the standard for such orders is simply too low.

Andrew C. McCarthy

A Response to Professor Swire

Professor Peter Swire's thoughtful response goes wrong in three major respects.

First, he gives short shrift to the national security threat. If we were not actually facing a public safety challenge, individual interests in the privacy of financial, medical, and reading records could sensibly be elevated. But national security is the highest public interest, and when it is truly threatened, as it is now, it makes no sense to give individual interests primacy over the public's need to have foreign enemies thoroughly checked—particularly when the Supreme Court has made plain that there are no expectations of privacy in third-party records.

This failing infects even the worthy concern over section 215's "gag rule." The desirability of openness as a check on government overreaching is unassailable if national security is not threatened. A public safety threat, however, requires reasonable balance between the public interest in disclosure and the reality that disclosure makes our enemies, to be blunt, more efficient at killing us. The appropriate balance is to presume that Justice Department personnel will perform their functions honorably, but to expect searching congressional oversight.

In reality, the vast majority of third-party subpoena recipients have no interest in disclosure. Given the stakes involved, any modification of the gag rule should put the onus on the few who do to explain why they should not remain mum. As for the suggestion that prosecution is an adequate check on irresponsible disclosures, that is classic pre-9/11 mindset. If a terror organization lives to kill another day because a subpoena recipient compromised an investigation, it will be cold comfort that the recipient can be prosecuted for obstruction of justice.

The second error is an inaccurate portrait of how government actually works. It begins the regulator's common failure to perceive that when government's hands are tied out of a hyper-fear of corrupt behavior, the only hands being tied belong to the honest people—the occasional rogue will be a rogue no matter what the rules are. Again, when public safety is at issue, it is perilous to hamper responsible officials in pursuit of an illusion that the few bad people will conform.

Further, there isn't time, in the information age, for investigators to be looking at everything we actually want them to look at. The thought that they have the time and inclination to snoop on people's private affairs systematically for illegitimate reasons is not reality, and is not an appropriate operating assumption. Watergate-era abuses are frequently raised in this context, betraying a counterfactual notion that we stopped growing in the 1970s. The executive branch knows that history, as does the Congress. Mindful of it, they perform and oversee. Complemented by the political check of the ballot box, this is our best assurance that the mistakes of the past will not recur.

Finally, the suggested regulations will not have the desired effect. They will merely chase investigations into the criminal justice system, where none of the oversight mechanisms inherent in section 215 exist. The claim that the criminal sphere somehow limits executive action because of a requirement "that a crime has been, is, or will be committed" is wrong. Grand juries may investigate on the rankest suspicion or even to satisfy themselves that no crime has been committed. Assuming arguendo that Justice Department practice could temper this limitless authority, the fact is that terrorist conspiracies (Al Qaeda, Hezbollah, etc.) are ongoing. Crimes are being committed, the criminal statutes are tremendously broad, and there simply is no matter remotely touching on terrorism that a grand jury is barred from investigating.

Peter P. Swire

The Last Word

Although Andrew McCarthy begins by describing my essay as "thoughtful," he unfortunately then descends into rhetoric that has been far too common in the debates about the PATRIOT Act: my writing reveals "a classic pre-9/11 mindset"; it gives "short shrift to the national security threat"; and the documented history of abuse in Watergate and other eras is irrelevant because "the executive branch knows that history" and so abuses of power won't happen again. In fact, as Mr. McCarthy knows, my short essay draws on a much longer law review article, and that article addresses each of those points in detail.

Let's sum up the debate on section 215. Mr. McCarthy and I agree that the law should be changed to allow lawyers to be contacted by the party who receives the order. We agree that the law should be changed to permit that party to go to court to seek to narrow an overbroad or unduly burdensome governmental request. (Although he does not address the issue, I hope he would agree that the same rights are appropriate for parties who are subject to National Security Letters.)

On the gag rule, Mr. McCarthy relies on executive branch restraint and congressional oversight. Under the gag rule as currently written, it is likely a crime for persons to tell Congress that they have been subject to a 215 order or National Security Letter. That leaves us with only executive branch self-restraint.

I have proposed a number of possible modifications to the gag rule. All of them are designed to provide public accountability while minimizing the likelihood of leaking information to terrorists. I try in my writings never to be alarmist. That said, the current gag rule is wildly outside of the American tradition and should be amended.

Section 218.
Amending the FISA Standard

Andrew C. McCarthy
David Cole

Summary

Mary DeRosa

Section 218 amends FISA by changing the certification requirement when the government seeks a FISA surveillance
or search order. Previously, the government was required to
certify that "the purpose" of the application was to obtain foreign
intelligence information. After section 218, the government must
certify that obtaining foreign intelligence information is "a significant purpose" of the application. This change was designed to promote information sharing between intelligence and law enforcement officials and to eliminate what has become known as the "wall"
that separated law enforcement and intelligence investigations.

The FISA, passed in 1978, sets forth procedures for the conduct
of electronic surveillance and physical searches for foreign intelligence purposes. Over the years, the Department of Justice interpreted
FISA's requirement that "the purpose" of collection be foreign intelligence to restrict the use of FISA collection procedures when a law
enforcement investigation was involved. The restriction was designed
to ensure that prosecutors and criminal investigators did not use FISA
to circumvent the more rigorous warrant requirements for criminal
cases. But law enforcement and foreign intelligence investigations

often overlap, and enforcing this separation between intelligence and law enforcement investigations—the "wall"—inhibited coordination of these investigations and the sharing of foreign intelligence information with law enforcement officials. The change to "significant purpose" was intended to clarify that no such separation is necessary.

It is not clear whether the change in section 218 was legally necessary to eliminate the "wall." The Department of Justice argued to the FISA Court of Review in 2002 that the original FISA standard did not require the restrictions that the Department of Justice imposed over the years, and the court appears to have agreed. This leaves the precise legal effect of a sunset of section 218 somewhat murky.

Andrew C. McCarthy

Why Section 218 Should Be Retained

No subordination of national security to hypothetical fears of civil liberties abuse was more emblematic of the pre-9/11 world than the metaphorical "wall" erected to obstruct the information flow between intelligence and criminal investigators.

Section 218 of the PATRIOT Act dismantled this construct by amending its literal underpinning—the basis for the ill-conceived "primary purpose" test by which FISA was misinterpreted for nearly a quarter-century—to disastrous effect. As the wall was founded on a skewed interpretation of law, section 218 was theoretically unnecessary. Nevertheless, it was entirely appropriate, and its enactment proved to be critical.

Post-9/11, discussions focus on explaining the genesis of the wall rather than defending it. Indeed, former Attorney General Janet Reno, on whose watch the wall was solidified in internal guidelines, testified to the 9/11 Commission that more critical to national security than realigning the intelligence community would be "to knock down walls, to promote the sharing of information, and to enhance collaboration in the fight against terrorism." And in 2002, the Foreign Intelligence Surveillance Court of Review, in its first ever opinion, provided a detailed explanation of the wall's fatal flaws.

The relevant history traces to the 1978 enactment of FISA (50 U.S.C. §§ 1801 et seq. (2000 ed.)). A reaction to Vietnam and Watergate era domestic-intelligence abuses, FISA authorizes a special federal FISA court to regulate and monitor the executive branch's conduct of electronic surveillance and physical searches in the context of national-security investigations. This is in contrast to ordinary investigations, where the use of those techniques is governed by the criminal law.

In the latter, agents must present probable cause of a crime to obtain a warrant. FISA, on the other hand, is not principally about rooting out crime; it is about national defense, targeting foreign enemies, including international terrorists. Thus, rather than requiring probable cause of a crime, FISA permitted government to "obtain foreign intelligence information" if "there is probable cause to believe that . . . the target of the electronic surveillance is a foreign power or an agent of a foreign power[.]"

The difficulty here is that any theoretical divide between criminal and intelligence matters would not track reality. Espionage, for example, is both a dire national security issue and a felony. Similarly, terrorists commit many crimes (e.g., immigration fraud, identity theft, money laundering, seditious conspiracy, possession of precursor explosives, and bombing, to name just a few) in the course of plotting and attacking. Thus, whether an agent's investigative authority comes from FISA or the criminal law, what emerges is evidence that constitutes both national security intelligence and proof of quotidian crimes.

This should pose no problem. Agents conducting a proper investigation uncover information. Free to compare notes and study multiple options for dealing with threats to public safety, they can wisely choose the approach that makes the most sense in light of the entire informational mosaic. Prosecution of a crime will get a dangerous person off the street and, equally important, may motivate him to cooperate about the inner workings of a terror network. On the other hand, sustained monitoring might reveal the nature of a terror enterprise while allowing government to prevent attacks without triggering disclosure obligations that attend a prosecution (which educate terrorists about the state and sources of government's intelligence). Plainly, national security dictates a fully informed strategy, taking advantage of the tactics that best fit the circumstances. Prior to 9/11, however, development of such a strategy was hamstrung by a hypothetical and wrong-headed concern: *viz.*, that permitting use in criminal cases of FISA-generated evidence might induce agents to resort to FISA when their "real" purpose was to conduct a criminal investigation.

This was irrational. First, the existence of a crime or national security threat is an objective reality, entirely independent of the investigators' subjective mindsets about why they are investigating. As for agent motivation, our concerns should be whether they have a good reason for investigating and whether the facts they present to a court are accurate. If those things are so, and agents happen to uncover evidence they did not anticipate finding, that is cause for celebration, not suppression. Thus, it has for decades been the law that (i) evidence of Crime A is admissible even if it was seized in the execution of a warrant based on probable cause of Crime B; but (ii) evidence of a crime is suppressed if the probable cause predicating its seizure was based on intentional misstatements of material fact.

Second, it is not sensible to suspect systematically dishonest resort to FISA. FISA applications require a specialized and rigorous internal approval process before presentation to the court. Assuming arguendo an agent willing to act corruptly, it would be far easier and less detectable to fabricate the evidence necessary to get an ordinary criminal wiretap than to fabricate a national security reason to use FISA.

Finally, FISA as written posed no obstacle to the use of FISA evidence for criminal prosecution. From a national security perspective, this made eminent sense given the aforementioned propensity of terrorists to commit crimes and the consequent centrality of prosecution as a means to win cooperation and thus secure vital intelligence.

Regrettably, this common sense came unmoored over time. FISA required that a high executive branch official—typically, the FBI director—represent that "the purpose" of the investigation was to obtain foreign-intelligence information (as opposed to building a prosecution). This was simply intended to be a certification; it did not purport to restrict either the scope of the investigation or the permissible uses of any resulting evidence. Unfortunately, soon after FISA took effect, the Justice Department began construing the certification not as a mere announcement of purpose but as something more restrictive: a substantive limitation on the use of FISA evidence in criminal cases.

As the Review Court opinion elaborated, over time this erroneous interpretation of the certification requirement led to a "false dichotomy": a futile endeavor to sort FISA-derived information into the purportedly distinct categories of mere intelligence and criminal evidence. Moreover, given the government's apparent fear that there might be impropriety in the acquisition of criminal evidence via FISA, it should have come as no surprise that the federal courts, too, began fashioning safeguards not found in FISA's text. Thus was born the "primary purpose" test, under which FISA-derived evidence could not be used in criminal prosecutions unless the government demonstrated that its primary purpose had been to collect intelligence, not build a criminal case.

To the contrary, as the Review Court held in 2002, FISA as enacted "clearly did not preclude or limit the government's use . . . of foreign intelligence information, which included evidence of certain kinds of criminal activity, in a criminal prosecution." (Emphasis in original.) But rather than challenge the primary purpose test, the Justice Department bolstered it, by internal 1995 regulations, into what became known as "the wall." This procedural edifice instructed "the FBI and Criminal Division [to] ensure that advice intended to preserve the option of a criminal prosecution does not inadvertently result in either the fact or the appearance of the Criminal Division's directing or controlling the [foreign intelligence (FI) or counterintelligence (FCI)] investigation toward law enforcement objectives."

This directive, the Review Court found, was "narrowly interpreted" to " prevent the FBI intelligence officials from communicating with the Criminal Division regarding ongoing FI or FCI investigations." This effectively cut intelligence investigators off not only from criminal agents but also from Assistant United States Attorneys who, by virtue of investigating and prosecuting several terrorism cases in the 1990s, were among the government's best resources regarding Al Qaeda and its affiliates.

The best-known pernicious consequence of all this occurred in August 2001. Relying on the wall, FBI headquarters declined to allow criminal investigators to assist an intelligence investigation seeking to locate probable terrorists Khalid al-Midhar and Nawaf al-Hazmi. A few weeks later, on 9/11, the pair helped hijack Flight 77 and pilot it into the Pentagon.

Section 218 makes a seemingly small but crucial adjustment: it guts the primary purpose test by requiring a government to certify that foreign intelligence is merely a significant purpose, rather than the purpose, for the FISA application. This strikes the correct balance: It recognizes that there is nothing inherently wrong with collecting criminal evidence by FISA, but ensures that FISA will not be employed unless there is some worthy national security purpose.

Section 218 was perhaps legally unnecessary. The Justice Department, after all, could, absent legislation, have changed its internal guidelines and argued that FISA had been misconstrued. Yet, it was certainly apt for Congress itself to address a key cog of pre-9/11 intelligence failure. Furthermore, given that the FISA court, post-9/11, improperly attempted to institute the wall procedures as an exercise of judicial supervision, it was no doubt immensely significant to the Court of Review—in reversing the FISA court in 2002—that the wall had been rejected not just by DOJ but by the force of law.

Section 218 is vital. The sunset should be removed, and the provision should otherwise remain as is.

David Cole

Imaginary Walls and Unnecessary Fixes

Supporters of the PATRIOT Act often complain that critics have perpetuated myths about the Act, blaming the Act for more than it actually deserves. But supporters are equally guilty of propagating competing myths in this debate, nowhere more so than with respect to section 218 and the "wall." Justice Department officials regularly credit section 218, as has Andrew McCarthy here, with bringing down a "wall" constructed by the Foreign Intelligence Surveillance Act (FISA) that barred information sharing between criminal law enforcement officials and intelligence agents. But as McCarthy himself concedes, FISA did not in fact require a "wall" before section 218 was enacted. As such, the amendment made by section 218 was neither necessary nor sufficient to eliminate the barriers to information sharing captured in the image of the "wall." There were many impediments to information sharing before 9/11, but their cause was and remains today largely bureaucratic, not statutory. Moreover, the reform that section 218 did actually make is of questionable constitutionality, because it permits searches undertaken primarily for criminal law purposes on less than the criminal probable cause showing that the Fourth Amendment requires for criminal law enforcement searches.

Section 218 made a very simple change to pre-existing law. Prior to the PATRIOT Act, FISA required that foreign intelligence gathering be "the purpose" of a FISA wiretap or search; section 218 requires that foreign intelligence gathering be only "a significant purpose" of a FISA wiretap or search. Courts had interpreted the pre-PATRIOT Act language to require the government to show that the "primary purpose" of a FISA application was intelligence gathering rather than criminal law enforcement. Critics often dismiss that distinction as silly, because, as McCarthy argues, many terrorist crimes are matters of both criminal law and foreign intelligence. But the pre-PATRIOT Act law recognized that, and in no way precluded FISA searches simply because they might also have a criminal law purpose. The "primary purpose" test simply sought to reduce the risk that FISA, which permits searches on less than criminal probable cause, would become an end run around the constitutional requirement of criminal probable cause for searches conducted for criminal law purposes. The law acknowledged that investigations might have dual purposes, but contemplated that if the government's primary purpose was criminal law enforcement, it should be required to seek a warrant under the criminal probable cause standard. As long as the government's primary purpose was foreign intelligence gathering, it could obtain a warrant under the less stringent FISA standards, even if the search also had criminal law enforcement purposes.

Contrary to myth, before section 218, FISA did not mandate a "wall" between law enforcement officials and intelligence agents. It did not bar prosecutors or law enforcement agents from turning over information to intelligence agents when the information might be relevant to foreign intelligence. Nor did it stop foreign intelligence agents from sharing with criminal prosecutors evidence of crime that they had discovered in their investigations, whether under FISA or otherwise. FISA never prohibited the government from using evidence obtained in a foreign intelligence investigation against a defendant in a criminal case. In fact, the government regularly relied upon FISA-obtained evidence in criminal trials before passage of the PATRIOT Act. Thus, claims that FISA created a "wall" are a myth.

Equally mythical are claims that section 218 made possible terrorist prosecutions that were not possible prior to its enactment. The Justice Department often points to the indictment of Sami Al-Arian, a University of South Florida professor accused of providing material support to the Palestinian Islamic Jihad, as an example of a prosecution it could bring only after section 218 was enacted.

But the government's case against Al-Arian is predicated on years of FISA wiretaps undertaken before the PATRIOT Act was enacted, and thus the validity of those wiretaps stands or falls under the pre-PATRIOT Act law, and is unaffected by section 218's relaxation of the standards for wiretaps conducted after the PATRIOT Act was enacted.

I do not mean to suggest that there were no impediments to information sharing before 9/11. There were plenty. But their principal source was not FISA, but administrative and bureaucratic culture. The FBI did not trust the CIA, and vice versa. Agencies were engaged in turf wars, and there were few if any mechanisms or incentives in place to break down the institutional boundaries between agencies. Legitimate concerns about not revealing sources make information sharing difficult even in the most well-organized operations. But the blame for these problems cannot be laid at the foot of FISA, and section 218 was not their solution.

It is true that the Justice Department had developed bureaucratic rules that erected further barriers to information sharing where FISA investigations were ongoing, in part out of concern that without such barriers, it would have difficulty showing that the primary purpose of a FISA investigation was foreign intelligence gathering. But those barriers were not required by statute, and appear to have been fed as much by the institutional barriers identified above as by any legitimate concerns about FISA's "primary purpose" test.

Critics of the wall sometimes suggest that before the PATRIOT Act, once a foreign intelligence investigation became primarily a criminal investigation, the government would have to take down the tap. But that is also not true. Once an investigation became primarily criminal in nature, government agents would simply have to satisfy the standards applicable to criminal investigations—namely, by showing that they had probable cause that the tap would reveal evidence of criminal conduct. The tap or the search could then continue. If an investigation has become primarily criminal in nature, it should not be too much to ask that the government show probable cause of criminal conduct to carry out a search or wiretap.

Indeed, the Constitution demands no less. FISA's constitutionality turns on an untested assumption (because the Supreme Court has never passed on the validity of FISA) that the government may engage in searches and wiretaps for foreign intelligence purposes on a lower showing of suspicion than is required for criminal law investigations. FISA does not require the government to show probable cause that evidence of a crime will be found, but only probable cause that the target of the search is an "agent of a foreign power." "Foreign power" is in turn defined so broadly that it encompasses any political organization comprised of a majority of noncitizens. Where "U.S. persons" are the target of a FISA search, the government must make additional showings, but to search the home of a foreign national here on a work permit, for example, the government need only show that he's an employee of an organization made up principally of noncitizens. It need not show that the individual be engaged in any criminal wrongdoing whatsoever, much less terrorism.

If FISA searches are constitutional, then, they must be justified on the basis of some application of the "administrative search" exception to the general Fourth Amendment rule requiring probable cause and a warrant for criminal law enforcement searches. That exception permits searches in limited settings on less than probable cause where the search serves some special need beyond criminal law enforcement. The FISA Court of Review relied on precisely this exception to find FISA searches valid. But the Supreme Court has carefully limited the "administrative search" exception to situations in which the government is pursuing a special need divorced from criminal law enforcement—e.g., highway or railroad safety, secondary school discipline, or enforcement of an administrative regime. It has refused to apply the exception where the government is engaged in criminal law enforcement, as in a checkpoint to search for cars carrying drugs. And the Court has also refused to apply the exception where the government has a "special need," but is using criminal law enforcement to further that need. Thus, it struck down a hospital program that subjected pregnant mothers to drug tests for the ultimate purpose of protecting the health of the fetus, where the hospital shared the test results with prosecutors in order to threaten the mothers with criminal prosecution if they did not seek drug treatment.

Where an investigation becomes primarily focused on criminal law enforcement, therefore, the "administrative search" exception no longer applies, and Supreme Court doctrine would compel the government to meet the traditional standards of criminal probable cause. Before the PATRIOT Act, FISA conformed to that requirement. By abandoning that distinction and allowing searches on less than probable cause where the government is primarily seeking criminal prosecution, section 218 raises a serious constitutional question. Thus, section 218 was not only unnecessary to bring down the wall, but may render FISA unconstitutional.

Finally, while claims that section 218 brought down the "wall" are greatly exaggerated, its enactment and other reforms have made it increasingly likely that information obtained through FISA wiretaps and searches will be used against defendants in criminal cases. In light of these developments, a useful reform at this point would be a provision permitting criminal defendants—or their cleared counsel—an opportunity to review the initial application for the FISA wiretap or search when contesting the admissibility of evidence obtained through a FISA search. Under current law, they have no such opportunity. Without access to the warrant application, defendants and their attorneys cannot meaningfully challenge the legality of the tap or search in the first place. And when government officials know that their actions will never see the light of day, they are more likely to be tempted to cut corners. An amendment requiring disclosure of FISA applications where evidence is sought to be used in a criminal trial would encourage adherence to the law by putting federal officials on notice that at some point the legality of the FISA warrant would be subjected to adversarial testing. Concerns about confidentiality could be met by limiting access to cleared counsel where necessary, and/or by applying the protections of the Classified Information Procedures Act. But there is no good reason for the current blanket exemption against the production of all such applications in criminal cases. The presumption should be in favor of adversarial testing where evidence is to be used in a criminal case.

Andrew C. McCarthy

A Response to Professor Cole

It is apt that Professor David Cole begins the title of his response "Imaginary Walls[.]" His submission is largely imaginary, creating rather than relating "myths" about the structural impediments to good intelligence that plagued the pre-9/11 world.

Professor Cole's response is thoroughly ill-conceived. His basic premise, section 218 aside, is that FISA itself is unconstitutional. Why? "[B]ecause the Supreme Court has never passed on [its] validity." This is an unworthy claim. As an act of Congress, FISA is presumptively valid. More to the point, it has been upheld repeatedly by federal appeals courts. The Supreme Court hasn't had to assess it lo these last 27 years because no challenge to it has been sufficiently colorable. By Cole's logic, we should fret that any makeweight claim may be of constitutional moment if its emptiness, unsurprisingly, has led the Supreme Court to eschew entertaining it.

Professor Cole's problem with FISA appears to be that his imaginary Fourth Amendment says searches are inappropriate absent probable cause of a crime. Of course, the actual Fourth Amendment prohibits only "unreasonable" searches, and the commission of crime is not a sine qua non of reasonableness. The American people obviously have a right to determine if non-Americans are engaged in covert intelligence gathering, or worse. The FISA search standard is not, as Cole insists, a "lower showing of suspicion" than is required in the criminal context; it is a different showing of suspicion—still requiring probable cause, but of foreign power agency rather than traditional crime.

The suggestion that a "foreign power" under FISA could be any "political organization" comprised predominantly of noncitizens is overwrought. One isn't told what Professor Cole means by a "political organization"—Hezbollah, Hamas, and Sinn Fein, for example, describe themselves as such—but the foreign powers FISA targets, by statutory definition, are those engaged in clandestine intelligence-gathering activities, sabotage or international terrorism. *See* 50 U.S.C. §§ 1801(b)(2)(A), (C).

Atop his faulty premise that FISA is suspect, Professor Cole piles the additional myth that section 218 is suspect because it permits FISA searches and surveillance "undertaken primarily for criminal law purposes." To the contrary, as the FISA Court of Review reasoned in its 2002 opinion, FISA as written never limited the government to searches whose primary purpose was intelligence gathering. By mandating that intelligence gathering be "a primary purpose," section 218 actually constrains the government in a way that neither the Fourth Amendment nor FISA does. Given that FISA easily passes Fourth Amendment muster, a provision such as section 218, which narrows it, a fortiori is not constitutionally suspect.

Finally, Professor Cole's mythical account skews the history of the wall and the purpose of section 218. Nobody is saying FISA "mandated a 'wall' between law enforcement officials and intelligence agents"—and when I argued that FISA did not require a wall, that palpably was an assertion, not, as Professor Cole oddly spins it, a "conce[ssion]." Yes, the wall was unnecessarily erected by the courts and the Justice Department. But that it was a mistake did not make it any less real. And that there may have been cultural impediments to intelligence sharing does not mean the structural ones manufactured by the wall were not critical.

Thus, to assert, as Cole does, that section 218 did not significantly contribute to prosecutions like the *Sami al-Arian* case because FISA wiretaps were valid under pre-PATRIOT law entirely misses the point. No one claims the wall tainted the propriety of intelligence gathering. It blocked sharing of the intelligence gathered. That is the bureaucratic monstrosity dismantled by section 218.

As a practical matter, section 218 was crucial because, had it not been enacted, the litigation ending in the FISA Court of Review decision would not have happened. Without that clarification of law, the disastrous primary purpose doctrine would be undisturbed, the unnecessary wall would still be in place, dots would remain unconnected, prosecutions like al-Arian would not have occurred, and the United States would be at considerably greater risk.

David Cole

More Myths

I did not argue that FISA, as amended by section 218, is unconstitutional simply because "the Supreme Court has never passed on [its] validity," as Andrew McCarthy claims, but because the very purpose of section 218's revision deprives FISA of its constitutional justification. FISA searches are generally defended as constitutional without probable cause of criminal activity because they fall under the "administrative search" exception to the probable cause requirement. But that exception, the Supreme Court has held, does not apply where the government's purpose is criminal law enforcement. FISA's pre-PATRIOT Act requirement that the search's primary purpose be foreign intelligence gathering, not criminal law enforcement, may well have been constitutionally required to make FISA searches valid. After the PATRIOT Act, foreign intelligence gathering need only be "a significant purpose" of the search—the primary purpose can be criminal law enforcement. That raises a serious constitutional concern.

McCarthy's only response is predicated on a demonstrably false premise. He says section 218 is constitutional because it "mandat[es] that intelligence gathering be 'a primary purpose'" of the investigation. In fact, the very purpose of section 218 was to eliminate the "primary purpose" requirement.

McCarthy's response is also erroneous in other respects. He falsely claims that FISA targets only those "foreign powers" engaged in intelligence gathering, sabotage or international terrorism, citing 50 U.S.C. sections 1801(b)(2)(A), (C)). In fact, FISA also defines "foreign power" as "a foreign-based political organization, not substantially composed of United States persons." 50 U.S.C. § 1801((a)(5). An "agent" of a foreign power need only be "an officer or employee of a foreign power." Neither agent nor power need be involved in any wrongdoing. Thus, a British citizen working here as an employee of Amnesty International is an "agent of a foreign power." Surely such a definition is a little overbroad.

Finally, McCarthy offers no response whatsoever to my proposal that, given FISA's increased use in criminal prosecutions, it should be amended to permit defendants in those prosecutions access to the FISA applications to challenge the warrant's validity. We may well need FISA, but FISA also needs to be held accountable to the adversary process, particularly as it becomes unmoored from its initial justification, and instead becomes an end-run around the Fourth Amendment in criminal investigations.

Intercepting Lone Wolf Terrorists

Michael J. Woods
Suzanne Spaulding

Summary

Mary DeRosa

Section 6001 of the Intelligence Reform and Terrorism Prevention Act of 2004, known as the "lone wolf" amendment, broadens FISA to allow surveillance of a new category of individuals. The provision amends FISA's definition of "agent of a foreign power" to include any person, other than a U.S. person, who "engages in international terrorism or activities in preparation therefore." Previously, that definition required a nexus to a foreign power or entity, such as a foreign government or an international terrorist organization. The expanded definition allows the government to use FISA for surveillance of a non-U.S. person who has no known ties to a group or entity. Congress passed this "lone wolf" provision because it was concerned that the previous FISA definitions did not cover unaffiliated individuals—or those for whom no affiliation can be established—who nonetheless engage or are preparing to engage in international terrorism.

The standards and procedures for FISA collection are different, more secretive, and in some cases less rigorous than those for law enforcement surveillance. But FISA is limited by its requirement that the target of surveillance be a foreign power or its agent. After this "lone wolf" provision, a target can be considered an "agent of a foreign power" without any evidence that they are acting with a group. But there must be probable cause that the target is engaging or preparing to engage in "international terrorism," which FISA defines to be activities that involve violent, criminal acts intended to intimidate or coerce a population or a government and that occur totally outside of the United States or transcend national boundaries.

Section 6001(b) of the Intelligence Reform Act subjects the "lone wolf" amendment to the PATRIOT Act's sunset provision. Therefore, unless reauthorized, the expanded authority will expire on December 31, 2005.

Michael J. Woods

Lone Wolf—Targeting the Loosely Affiliated Terrorist

Critics of FISA's new "lone wolf" provision argue it is a dangerous expansion of authority, allowing the application of FISA to individuals lacking any connection to foreign powers. The language actually enacted, however, integrates a definition of "international terrorism" that preserves a sufficiently strong foreign nexus requirement. Therefore, the statute's parts, taken together and read in context, contain adequate safeguards to ensure that the lone wolf provision will be used against its intended targets—international terrorists.

Before the lone wolf provision, there were two principal paths to obtain FISA surveillance of an international terrorist: first, by demonstrating probable cause that the target acts in the U.S. as a "member" of an international terrorist group (found in FISA section 101(b)(1)(A)); and second, by demonstrating probable cause that the target "knowingly engages in sabotage or international terrorism, or activities that are in preparation therefor, for or on behalf of a foreign power" (section 101(b)(2)(C)). The first option is difficult to establish given the informality of terrorist organizations and is not available where the target is a U.S. person. The second is the stock from which the present "lone wolf" provision is cut, and provides the conceptual foundation for the new provision.

The legislative history of those two original FISA provisions, found primarily in House Report 95-1283, Senate Report 95-701, and House Conference Report 95-1720, reveals that the drafters' chief concern here was to avoid application of the FISA to purely domestic terrorists or political dissidents. Congress was reacting to the Supreme Court's 1972 holding in *United States v. United States District Court* (found at 407 U.S. 297, and commonly called the "Keith case") that "domestic security surveillance" was subject to the warrant and reasonableness requirements of the Fourth Amendment. The group at issue in Keith was a radical organization (the White Panther Party) that had bombed a number of federal facilities to draw attention to the group's domestic social/political agenda. (*See The Court Legacy*, Vol. XI, No. 4 (Nov. 2003).) The Court emphasized that its Keith holding addressed only "the domestic aspects of national security" and did not reach "the activities of foreign powers or their agents." FISA was the legislative approach to the area beyond Keith: the field of foreign intelligence surveillance. In addressing terrorism as a national security threat, the FISA drafters needed to draw a line between the purely domestic variety covered by the Keith ruling and the activities of international terrorist organizations (which could take place in the United States).

After examining several different ways to describe terrorism, Congress drew that line by defining "international terrorism" in FISA (section 101(c)). That definition has three elements: first, the activities in question must involve violent acts that are a violation of U.S. criminal law (or would be if committed in U.S. jurisdiction); second, that the apparent purpose of the activities is to intimidate civilian populations or governments; and third, that the activities either occur outside of the U.S. or "transcend national boundaries" in terms of their means of execution, intended targets, or location of the perpetrators. The legislative history shows that Congress acknowledged that domestic groups could meet this definition if they acted internationally, or "receive[d] direction or substantial support" from a foreign terrorist group, but FISA could not be used in the absence of such information. Moreover, the fact that domestic activities were "parallel to or consistent with the desires of a foreign power" was insufficient to satisfy the definition. Protected speech ("mere sympathy for, identity of interest with, or vocal support for" a foreign-based terrorist group) was also insufficient. Thus, a strong link to foreign power activity, as well as a required showing of preparation for violent criminal acts, is embedded in the FISA definition of "international terrorism."

The new lone wolf provision descends from the existing definition of a U.S. person agent of a foreign power found in section 101(b)(2)(C) (a person who "knowingly engages in sabotage or international terrorism, or activities that are in preparation therefor, for or on behalf of a foreign power"), but differs in two key ways. First, the lone wolf provision drops the "knowingly" requirement because the lone wolf definition applies only to non-U.S. persons (and non-U.S. person FISA provisions do not include a scienter requirement). Second, the lone wolf provision lacks the final phrase "for or on behalf of a foreign power." The 1978 legislative history of that phrase (in sharp contrast to the detailed discussion of the "international terrorism" definition) only points out that it requires an explicit identification of the target's "knowing connection" to a group engaged in international terrorism. The elimination of this final phrase is less consequential than generally imagined because the "foreign nexus" requirement flows not just from the "for or on behalf of a foreign power" codicil but also (and perhaps more powerfully) from the "international terrorism" definition that remains incorporated into the lone wolf provisions. That definition continues to ensure that FISA is not applied to purely domestic political activity (even to domestic political violence). Therefore, the lone wolf provision addresses the fairly narrow factual scenario in which the government can demonstrate probable cause that the proposed FISA target is engaged in international terrorism but cannot demonstrate an agency relationship with an identifiable international terrorist group.

There are a number of situations in which this scenario might arise. The target could be espousing transnational approaches (like "universal jihad") without indicating allegiance to, or having contact with, any particular group. Perhaps the government's information links the target to a group, but those facts simply do not rise to the level of probable cause. The target could be linked to a previously unknown group for which government cannot yet meet every element of the FISA "foreign power" definition. There might be old information associating the target with a foreign group, but uncertainty as to the target's current allegiance (a key fact, given that the use of the present tense in the definition implies currency). A target could have contacts with several groups, but with no one connection rising to the level of probable cause. None of these scenarios would seem to be commonplace; and it is easy to imagine that a few additional facts would push the matter into the scope of the existing definitions. However, the category defined in the lone wolf provision, though small, does represent a gap and raises the question of whether or not an expanded FISA definition tailored to this particular factual range is justified.

Although the *Moussaoui* case is named most often as the justification for the lone wolf provision, it is now nearly impossible to examine those facts without the distortion of post-9/11 hindsight. A better, and more enduring, case for the change arises from the evolving nature of Al Qaeda. Even a cursory reading of the FISA reveals its presumption for state or quasi-state foreign powers. Although the FISA materials acknowledge that international terrorist groups are less formal and more fluid than foreign intelligence services, the 1970s-era groups that pop up as examples in the legislative history (the Baader-Meinhof Group, the Japanese Red Army, various Palestinian groups) were all relatively structured, often quasi-military, organizations. Subsequent generations of terrorists have learned that hierarchical organizations are well-established targets for western-style intelligence and law enforcement. By eschewing such structures, the new terrorists deprive us of the familiar terrain and build up their asymmetric advantage. The development of Al Qaeda from an initially traditional extremist group to a trans-cultural (and increasingly trans-sectarian) extremist movement is a sobering example of this evolution. Writing in *Foreign Affairs* (July/August 2003, "The Protean Enemy"), Jessica Stern described the rise of a "leaderless resistance" model in Al Qaeda, with extremist Web sites now offering tips on creating "clandestine activity cells" and promoting a "culture of jihad." In these conditions, it is more likely that situations falling within the factual band addressed by the lone wolf provision will occur. Rather than attempting to stretch outmoded definitions to cover these developments, the new language in FISA simply closes a definitional gap in our ability to deploy FISA in response to the present threat.

Finally, though often cited as an alternative, the availability of the criminal process to address the lone wolf scenario does not undermine the necessity of the new language. While the USA PATRIOT Act certainly removed barriers to the use of criminal investigative tools in the intelligence context, it did not alter the fundamental limitations of the criminal process regarding the protection of sensitive sources and methods. If the factual predication for a lone wolf scenario is drawn from sources that cannot be introduced into the criminal process (for example, information from a sensitive human source or from a foreign intelligence service), the criminal process is, in practical terms, unavailable. In such cases, FISA authority should be available, as it is for the other fact patterns addressed by its definitions. Given the required connection to a legitimate national security threat embedded in the FISA definition of "international terrorism," the new lone wolf language is both appropriately tailored within the existing parameters of foreign intelligence surveillance and justified by the evolving nature of our present adversary.

Suzanne Spaulding

"If It Ain't Broke, Don't Fix It"

The common wisdom—"if it ain't broke, don't fix it"—was ignored when Congress enacted the "lone wolf" amendment to the Foreign Intelligence Surveillance Act (FISA), allowing its use against an individual acting totally alone, with no connection to any foreign power, as long as they are "engaged in international terrorism or activities in preparation therefor." The result needlessly undermines the policy and constitutional justification for this very important national security tool.

The lone wolf provision is often referred to as the "Moussaoui fix." Although it had been floating around previously, the amendment came to the forefront only after the attacks of September 11, 2001, when the misperception took hold that FISA's requirements prevented the FBI from gaining access to a computer used by Zacharias Moussaoui, who was alleged at one time to be the 20th hijacker. In fact, the problem was not with the FISA statute but with the FBI's misinterpretation of the statute. This conclusion is supported by the findings of the Joint Congressional Intelligence Committee Inquiry into the 9/11 Attacks, an exhaustive Senate Judiciary Committee inquiry, and the 9/11 Commission.

In order to obtain a FISA order authorizing access to Moussaoui's computer, the FBI needed to show probable cause to believe that Moussaoui was acting "for or on behalf of a foreign power." A foreign power is defined to include a group engaged in international terrorism. As the Senate Judiciary Committee Report explained, the FBI misunderstood the FISA requirement:

[K]ey FBI personnel responsible for protecting our country against terrorism did not understand the law. The SSA [Supervisory Special Agent] at FBI Headquarters responsible for assembling the facts in support of the Moussaoui FISA application testified before the Committee in a closed hearing that he did not know that "probable cause" was the applicable legal standard for obtaining a FISA warrant. In addition, he did not have a clear understanding of what the probable cause standard meant. . . . In addition to not understanding the probable cause standard, the SSA's supervisor (the Unit Chief) responsible for reviewing FISA applications did not have a proper understanding of the legal definition of the "agent of a foreign power" requirement. Specifically, he was under the incorrect impression that the statute required a link to an already identified or "recognized" terrorist organization, an interpretation that the FBI and the supervisor himself admitted was incorrect.

FBI Oversight in the 107th Congress by the Senate Judiciary Committee: FISA Implementation Failures, An Interim Report by Senators Patrick Leahy, Charles Grassley & Arlen Specter (February 2003) at p. 17.

The Judiciary Committee Report notes that while "a group" is not defined in FISA, "in common parlance, and using other legal principles, including criminal conspiracy, a group consists of two or more persons whether identified or not." Moreover, remember that the FBI does not have to "prove" the target's connection to a terrorist group. They must merely meet the "probable cause" standard, which, as the Judiciary Committee Report points out, does not mean "more likely than not" or "an over 51% chance," but "only the probability and not a prima facie showing." The Report concluded that "there appears to have been sufficient evidence in the possession of the FBI which satisfied the FISA requirements for the Moussaoui application" (p. 23). Thus, no "fix" was required to search Moussaoui's computer.

Moreover, the FBI could very likely have obtained a criminal warrant to search Moussaoui's computer. They did not pursue that because they were concerned that doing so would preclude them from getting a FISA warrant later if they were turned down for the criminal warrant or ultimately did develop what they thought was sufficient information linking him to a terrorist group. This concern was based on the "primary purpose" test—viewed as precluding the use of FISA if the primary purpose was criminal prosecution rather than intelligence collection—which was subsequently changed in the USA PATRIOT Act. With the PATRIOT Act change, and in light of a subsequent opinion by the Foreign Intelligence Surveillance Court of Review, this would no longer be a concern, and the government could seek a criminal warrant without concern of precluding future use of FISA. Moreover, because of the post-9/11 enactment of broad criminal statutes related to terrorism, in virtually every case in which you could meet the probable cause standard for obtaining a FISA warrant for a lone wolf ("engages in international terrorism activities or activities in preparation therefor"), you could meet the probable cause standard for a criminal warrant. Nor would the need to use sensitive information in the application be a compelling concern, given that classified information is shared with judges in other criminal contexts, such as pursuant to the Classified Intelligence Procedures Act.

One might argue that no matter how rare the instances might be in which FISA may be the best way to go after a lone wolf, we should include this option in the law "just in case." The problem with this reasoning is that it comes at a high cost. In addition to being unnecessary, the lone wolf provision undermines the policy and constitutional justification for FISA. When Congress enacted FISA, it carefully limited its application in order "to ensure that the procedures established in [FISA] are reasonable in relation to legitimate foreign counterintelligence requirements and the protected rights of individuals. Their reasonableness depends, in part, upon an assessment of the difficulties of investigating activities planned, directed, and supported from abroad by foreign intelligence services and foreign-based terrorist groups." Senate Report 95-701, at 14-15.

The congressional debate, and the court cases that informed and followed it, clearly reflect the sense that this limited exception from the normal criminal warrant requirements was justified only when dealing with foreign powers or their agents. The exception was not based simply on a foreign nexus; it did not apply to every non-U.S. person whose potentially dangerous activity transcended U.S. borders. The Fourth Circuit Court of Appeals has emphasized that the exception is justified "only when the object of the search or the surveillance is a foreign power, its agent or collaborators. In such cases, the government has the greatest need for speed, stealth, and secrecy, and the surveillance in such cases is most likely to call into play difficult and subtle judgments about foreign and military affairs." (*United States v. Truong Dinh Hung*, 629 F.2d 908, *cert. denied,* 454 U.S. 1144 (1982).)

Individuals acting entirely on their own simply do not implicate the level of "foreign and military affairs" that justify the use of this extraordinary foreign intelligence tool. Congress has authorized the use of military force against the terrorists who carried out the attacks of September 11 and those acting on their behalf—not against individuals acting alone with absolutely no connection to any terrorists.

And while there are obvious foreign policy implications of targeting an individual with ties to an international terrorist group, it is not clear why an individual acting alone raises any more significant foreign policy concerns than would targeting any other foreign criminal inside the United States.

The requirement that the lone wolf must be "engaged in international terrorism or acts in preparation therefor" does not solve this problem. Nowhere in FISA's definition of "international terrorism" is there any requirement for a connection to a foreign government or terrorist group. Nor is such a requirement embedded in the definition by virtue of the legislative history. In fact, report language emphasizing the need for a direct link to a foreign power simply further highlights the importance of that element in the overall legislative framework that Congress had carefully constructed.

Perhaps it was Congress's understanding that the legitimacy of FISA depends upon a nexus to a foreign power that led to its strange decision last year to "fix" FISA by slipping the "lone wolf" into the definition of "agents of a foreign power." However, by defining an individual acting totally alone, with no connection to any other individual, group, or government, as "an agent of a foreign power," Congress moved beyond Orwell into the logic of Humpty Dumpty: "When I use a word, it means just what I choose it to mean." Unfortunately, this legislative legerdemain stretched the logic of this important statutory tool to a point that threatens its legitimacy. If its use against a true lone wolf is ever challenged in court, FISA, too, may have a great fall.

Michael J. Woods

Response

Ms. Spaulding argues that we should reject the "lone wolf" amendment because it is allegedly unnecessary, and it would undermine the "policy and constitutional justification for FISA" to create a provision applicable to future terrorists that cannot be proved to be affiliated with a terrorist group. But wait—the purpose of FISA is the collection of foreign intelligence information, defined as "information that relates to . . . the ability of the United States to protect against actual or potential attacks" and "sabotage or international terrorism." *See* 50 U.S.C. § 1801. The new "lone wolf" FISAs, like all FISAs, are available only if the government can certify that the information sought is foreign intelligence. If the government can meet the "international terrorism" and "foreign intelligence information" requirements, how could the "level of foreign or military affairs" not be implicated? And why should the government then forego its purpose-made intelligence capability (FISA) in favor of ad hoc criminal tools? Who does such a limitation actually protect?

As for the constitutional foundations of FISA, Ms. Spaulding cites the *Truong* decision, which, despite its date, addresses a pre-FISA case. The quoted *Truong* language refers not to FISA, but to fully warrantless activities conducted at the sole discretion of the executive branch. FISA, of course, does not fall into that category, as the Foreign Intelligence Court of Review explained at length in its 2002 opinion (and as the *Truong* court itself recognized in footnote 4). The "lone wolf" provision just allows the government to obtain foreign intelligence about a non-U.S. person who is engaged in international terrorism, and to do this under the authority and direct supervision of a court expressly created to keep the domestic collection of foreign intelligence within constitutional limits.

Criminal warrants are poor substitutes for FISA. The criminal justice system has a very limited, and highly contingent, ability to protect classified information. The Classified Information Procedures Act, for example, applies only after criminal charges have been filed, and thus doesn't help with getting search warrants. Relying on a judge to seal records is, at best, a temporary solution, unsuited to the long-term protection of intelligence sources. Sometimes those sources are foreign governments unwilling to expose their own intelligence information to the unpredictability of our criminal courts. FISA was designed to accommodate all of these concerns, and functions very well in this regard.

Ms. Spaulding also argues that the lone wolf provision is unnecessary because we could have used FISA on Moussaoui anyway (since it turns out he really wasn't a lone wolf). Of course, some of the key information relied on by the Judiciary Committee in reaching its conclusion was not actually known to the relevant FBI officials prior to 9/11. Unlike post-event investigators, counterterrorism agents don't have the benefit of flawless hindsight. Uncertainty is their natural habitat and their tools should be built to function in that environment. Moreover, the lone wolf amendment isn't about Moussaoui. Counterterrorism agents need the tools to stop the next would-be terrorist, not the last one.

Suzanne Spaulding

A Possible Compromise

The FISA Court of Review (FISCR) cited the statute's purpose, "to protect the nation against terrorists and espionage threats directed by foreign powers," to conclude that FISA searches, while not clearly meeting "minimum Fourth Amendment warrant standards," are nevertheless reasonable. Because the definitions of "foreign intelligence" and "international terrorism" do not include this necessary nexus to a foreign power, they do not solve the constitutional and policy issues raised when applying FISA to a true lone wolf. Nor should we rely upon FISA judges to ensure that an overly broad standard is only applied in ways that are sensible; the law makes clear that their role is simply ensuring that the standards set forth in the statute are met.

Congress should let the lone wolf provision sunset and instead address perceived (although unproven) concerns about having to show foreign power connections by creating a permissive presumption that if there is probable cause to believe that a non-U.S. person is engaged in or preparing for international terrorist activities, he or she can be considered an agent of a foreign power. If it ultimately becomes clear that the target is acting alone, a criminal warrant should be sought. Who does this constitutional safeguard protect? All of us.

Other Expiring Provisions

Stewart Baker

Some of the PATRIOT Act's provisions are set to expire in 2005 but weren't controversial at the time the Act was approved. As far as we can tell, they still aren't. We were unable to find contributors on either side of the PATRIOT debate who were interested in spending time and ink to argue about the following seven provisions. Not surprisingly, it is difficult to understand why some of the provisions are due to sunset at all.

Section 201: Authority to Intercept Wire, Oral, and Electronic Communications Relating to Terrorism

Not all crimes are serious enough to justify a voice wiretap, or so Congress decided in 1968. The government can only wiretap voice communications to gather evidence about felonies that Congress has designated as wiretap-worthy. After September 11, there was a rush to make sure that every terrorism-related felony was on the wiretap list.

Section 201 allows wiretaps when the government is investigating attacks on Americans outside the United States, use of certain weapons of mass destruction, acts of terrorism transcending national boundaries, financial transactions with a government that sponsors terrorism, the provision of material support to terrorists, and the provision of material support to designated terrorist organizations, as well as chemical weapons crimes. Since wiretaps are highly productive and often essential in terrorism cases, there has been no controversy over section 201.

Section 202: Authority to Intercept Wire, Oral, and Electronic Communications Relating to Computer Fraud and Abuse Offenses

Section 202, like section 201, adds to the list of wiretap-worthy felonies. It allows voice wiretaps in the investigation of computer fraud and abuse (aka hacking). Wiretaps have long been used in hacking cases because in the case of data wiretaps, Congress declared that any federal felony was wiretap-worthy. But when hackers started using new Voice over Internet Protocol to mix voice and data while hacking, prosecutors worried that the "wiretap-worthy" requirement might be applied to hacking intercepts.

Section 202 solves that problem by allowing voice taps in hacking investigations. While section 202 doesn't have an obvious connection to terrorism (at least not until we suffer our first serious politically motivated hacking attacks), the change is such an inside-baseball modification that no one who understands it seems particularly exercised by it.

Section 204: Clarification of Intelligence Exceptions From Limitations on Interception and Disclosure of Wire, Oral, and Electronic Communications

The United States more or less invented the idea of spies who obey the law. (They break foreign law, of course, but they're not supposed to violate U.S. law.) That turns out to be a bit tricky, though, when Congress writes broad criminal statutes that could apply abroad to the sorts of things that intelligence agencies do routinely—like wiretap foreigners. To make sure that some future special prosecutor doesn't go after intelligence officers who were just doing their jobs, Congress has written a special "intelligence agency" exception to its criminal prohibition on wiretapping. Of course, it has to amend the exception whenever it gives the agencies new wiretap authority.

Section 204 does just that; it adds intelligence agency pen registers and intercepts of electronic communications to the "intelligence-gathering" exception. This should be totally uncontroversial. Even people who object to allowing intelligence-agency pen registers or electronic intercepts should be focusing their fire on the provision that allows such intrusions, not on a provision that simply clarifies that the law does not simultaneously permit and prohibit the same act.

Section 207: Duration of FISA Surveillance of Non-United States Persons Who Are Agents of a Foreign Power

All good things come to an end, and FISA intercept orders are no exception to the rule. They can be renewed, of course, but in the wake of September 11, a massive increase in the number of FISA orders led to breakdowns in the office that drafts and processes the orders. There were apparently wiretap targets whose intercepts were allowed to lapse, not because the targets were no longer targets but because the paperwork couldn't be processed fast enough.

Section 207 addresses this problem by extending the duration of FISA orders for certain non-U.S. persons who are agents of a foreign power. The section extends the maximum surveillance period to 120 days and the maximum physical search period to 90 days, both with longer extensions possible when the target is an agent of a foreign power. Because it is not aimed at U.S. persons and does not tinker with the general standards governing FISA surveillance, this is a fairly uncontroversial way to spare government resources by avoiding the constant need for renewal applications.

Indeed, the latest set of intelligence reform proposals, from the Robb-Silberman Commission on Weapons of Mass Destruction, seems to suggest that further extensions are desirable. Thus, any controversy in this area may relate to Administration efforts to extend further the deadline for renewing FISA orders against non-U.S. persons.

Section 217: Interception of Computer Trespasser Communications

When the owner of a computer system finds a hacker on that system, the owner has full authority to watch the hacker's activities. The hacker can't claim that his privacy was invaded, any more than a burglar could object if a homeowner spied on him from the top of the stairs. Oddly, though, the hacker might have a privacy claim if the system owner calls in the police and lets them watch what the hacker is doing. Arguably, in that case, the police are using the system owner as their agent in the execution of a wiretap of the hacker—and doing so without a court order.

If you think that's pretty far-fetched, you won't have much trouble with section 217, which allows the authorities to intercept the inbound and outbound communications of a computer hacker once they have the consent of the owner of the hacked system. It doesn't have much to do with terrorism as we've known it so far, of course, but it has also proven quite uncontroversial.

Section 223: Civil Liability for Certain Unauthorized Disclosures

Section 223 makes government officers liable for unlawful disclosure or use of information gained from wiretaps, and it confirms the right of government agencies to discipline employees for willful or intentional violations of federal wiretap or stored communications law. Section 223 also imposes civil liability on the United States for willful violations of federal wiretap law, stored communications law, and FISA law, regarding surveillance, physical searches, or the use or installation of pen registers or trap and trace devices.

Prosecutors and police would be perfectly happy to see this provision expire, but civil libertarians presumably want it renewed. In any event, no one is making much of an issue about it, so section 223 likely will be renewed without a fight.

Section 225: Immunity for Compliance With FISA Wiretap

When a phone company or Internet service provider helps the police carry out a regular law-enforcement wiretap, the company is given immunity from suit as long as it acts in good faith. This has long been a feature of intercept law, with one exception. FISA, which authorizes intelligence wiretaps, doesn't give a legislative immunity to third parties who help the government carry out the intercept. Maybe when FISA was drafted, no one expected spies to bring privacy lawsuits. Or maybe it was just an oversight.

In any event, Congress finally got around to repairing the gap in section 225 of the USA PATRIOT Act, granting the standard legislative immunity to phone companies, ISPs, landlords, and others who help effectuate FISA orders. Since these third parties could probably have claimed a common-law privilege anyway, the statute was more in the nature of a clarification, and it's hard to see why section 225 was put on the sunset list in the first place. I may be biased here (I've represented ISPs in FISA wiretap matters), but I suspect that the only controversy over section 225 is whether the provision should be made permanent, rather than held hostage in future sunset debates.

The provisions outlined above are uncontroversial for a variety of reasons—they are designed to fix oversights of previous statutes, have only a tangential relationship (thus far) to terrorism, or merely attempt to promote government efficiency. While congressional debates often take odd turns for reasons other than the substantive issue being debated, these provisions are likely to be renewed with little attention. If that turns out to be the case, perhaps some consideration should be given to making these provisions a permanent part of the criminal code.

Part Two
Other Issues

Section 213.
"Sneak and Peek" Search Warrants

Heather Mac Donald
James X. Dempsey

Summary

Mary DeRosa

Section 213, known as the "sneak and peek" provision, authorizes delayed notice of the execution of criminal search warrants. Section 213 is not subject to the PATRIOT Act's sunset provision. Previously, there was no statutory authorization for clandestine searches of private premises in criminal investigations, although FISA permitted such searches for national security purposes. Courts have allowed delayed-notice searches, however, in a number of criminal cases beginning in the 1980s. Most of these cases involved only the clandestine seizure of intangible evidence (e.g., information or photographs), not tangible property. Section 213 amends 18 U.S.C. section 3103a, which relates to warrants for the search and seizure of evidence of federal crimes, to permit these "sneak and peek" searches. This new authority is not limited to terrorism; it permits delayed-notice searches for any federal crime.

To obtain a "sneak and peek" warrant, the government must give the court "reasonable cause" to believe that providing notice of the search would have an dverse result. An adverse result is defined as (1) endangering a person's life or physical safety, (2) flight from prosecution, (3) destruction of or tampering with evidence, (4) intimidation of potential witnesses, or (5) otherwise seriously jeopardizing an investigation or unduly delaying a trial. Section 213 permits the warrant to authorize clandestine seizure of tangible property when the court specifically finds that such seizure is "reasonably necessary." A "sneak and peek" warrant under section 213, must provide for notice to the subject "within a reasonable time of its execution, which period may thereafter be extended by the court for good cause shown."

Heather Mac Donald

Sneak-and-Peek in the Full Light of Day

There is no better place to dissect anti-PATRIOT Act demagoguery than in the furor around section 213. All the rhetorical techniques used by PATRIOT Act critics—"Conceal Legal Precedent," "Hide the Judge," "Amend the Statute," and, most profoundly, "Reject Secrecy"— come together in the attack on this provision.

Here's how section 213 works: Let's say an FBI agent has evidence that a Saudi chemical engineering student in Virginia has been communicating with possible jihadists in Yemen about a local chlorine plant. The Bureau wants to examine the Saudi's computer for evidence of a nascent plot to blow up the facility. However, if the agent shows up at the chemist's door with a warrant to search his hard drive, he will disclose the investigation. The Saudi, if he is indeed a terrorist, will alert his fellow cell members in this country as well as abroad. The cell will destroy evidence of a plot whose investigation could have unlocked a major wing of Al Qaeda. Notifying the Saudi of the government's interest could also put the FBI's lead informant, a Pakistani engineer in Maryland, at risk.

Rather than jeopardizing this major terror investigation, the FBI asks the judge who is issuing the computer search warrant to delay notice of the search to the Saudi. Section 213 allows the judge to grant the delay if he finds "reasonable cause" to believe that notice would result in death or physical harm to an individual, flight from prosecution, evidence tampering, witness intimidation, or other serious jeopardy to an investigation. In this case, the judge will likely allow a delay, since notice could seriously jeopardize the investigation, and would likely result in evidence tampering and witness intimidation.

The delay of notice under section 213 is only temporary, however. The government must eventually notify the Saudi that his computer has been searched "within a reasonable period."

Section 213 carefully balances traditional expectations of notice and the imperatives of preemptive terror and crime investigations. That's not how left- and right-wing libertarians have portrayed it, however. They present section 213, which they have dubbed "sneak-and-peek," as one of the most outrageous new powers seized by former Attorney General John Ashcroft. The ACLU's fundraising pitches warn: "Now, the government can secretly enter your home while you're away . . . rifle through your personal belongings . . . download your computer files . . . and seize any items at will. . . . And, because of the PATRIOT Act, you may never know what the government has done." Richard Leone, president of the Century Foundation and editor of *The War on Our Freedoms: Civil Liberties in an Age of Terrorism*, cites the fact that the PATRIOT Act "allows the government to conduct secret searches without notification" to support his hyperbolic claim that the Act is "arguably the most far-reaching and invasive legislation passed since the Espionage Act of 1917 and the Sedition Act of 1918."

These claims are wrong, but usefully so, since they draw on rhetorical strategies that PATRIOT Act critics endlessly employ against other provisions of the Act. Discredit the following strategies here and you have the key for discrediting the entire anti-PATRIOT propaganda machine.

Conceal Legal Precedent

The idea that section 213 is a radical new power is a rank fabrication. For decades, federal courts have allowed investigators to delay notice of a search in drug cases, organized crime, and child pornography, for the same reasons as in section 213. Indeed, the ability to delay notice of a search is an almost inevitable concomitant of investigations that seek to stop a crime before it happens. But the lack of precise uniformity in the court rulings on delayed notice slowed down complex national terror cases. Section 213 codified existing case law under a single national standard to streamline detective work; it did not create new authority regarding searches. Those critics who believe that the target of a search should always be notified prior to the search, regardless of the risks, should have raised their complaints decades ago—to the Supreme Court and the many other courts that have recognized the necessity of a delay option.

Hide the Judge

The cascades of anti-section 213 vitriol contain not one mention of the fact that the FBI can only delay notice of a search pursuant to judicial approval. Instead, the opponents suggest that under section 213, the government can unilaterally and for the most nefarious of purposes decide to conceal its investigative activities. There is no greater check on arbitrary government power than judicial review; for that reason, the PATRIOT Act is shot through with judicial review requirements. Good luck finding any acknowledgment of these constitutional checks in the PATRIOT Act diatribes, however.

Indeed, the ACLU implies that federal investigators can not only unilaterally delay notice, but can choose what and whether to search, without any judicial oversight: "Now, the government can . . . seize any items [from your home] at will," it blares. But section 213 allows a warrant to issue only if a judge finds a "reasonable necessity" for it—the executive's arbitrary "will" has nothing to do with it.

Amend the Statute

Anti-PATRIOT lore has it that section 213 allows the government to permanently conceal a search. The section "allows the government to conduct secret searches without notification," cries Richard Leone. This conceit rewrites the section, which provides only for a delay of notice, not its cancellation. A warrant issued under section 213 must explicitly require notice after a "reasonable" period of time. This key feature of the section is completely suppressed by the critics.

Reject Secrecy

Most of the attacks on the PATRIOT Act emanate from a single source: the critics do not believe that the government should ever act in secret. In their world, if the FBI has received a tip about a possible Al Qaeda cell in Phoenix that may be planning to detonate a dirty bomb in Las Vegas, the Bureau should seek a wiretap warrant in open court, with notification to the cell members. If intelligence agents want to search the group's apartments, they should inform the cell in advance to give them an opportunity to challenge the search. Court TV could broadcast the legal wrangling between the cell's attorneys and intelligence agents; legal experts could provide running commentary about the likely scope of the FBI's investigations.

This transparent approach may satisfy those on the left and right who believe that the American people have no greater enemy than their own government, but it fails to answer the major question: how would it possibly be effective in protecting the country? The PATRIOT Act critics fail to grasp the distinction between the prosecution of an already committed crime, for which notice requirements were primarily crafted, and the effort to preempt a catastrophic attack on American soil before it happens. For preemptive investigations, secrecy is of the essence. Opponents of the PATRIOT Act have never explained how they think the government can track down the web of Islamist activity in public. Given that section 213 and other sections are carefully circumscribed with judicial checks and balances, it is in fact the secrecy that they allow that most riles the opponents.

Congress should not listen to such misguided attacks. Section 213 is not a new power, it is not an unchecked power, it is not a permanent power. Temporary secrecy during a preemptive investigation, executed pursuant to judicial oversight, is constitutional and indispensable.

James X. Dempsey

Reply

Section 213 is a perfect example of a good idea gone too far. It is also a perfect example of how the PATRIOT Act has been used in an effort to expand government powers, without suitable checks and balances, in areas having nothing to do with terrorism. Finally, it illustrates how, when rhetoric is left behind, it is possible to frame appropriate checks and balances for what, by any definition, are some especially intrusive powers.

As a starting point, of course, in serious investigations of international terrorists, the government should be able to act with secrecy. But guess what proponents of section 213 never mention? In international terrorism investigations, even before the PATRIOT Act, the government already had the authority to carry out secret searches. The Foreign Intelligence Surveillance Act was amended in 1994 to allow secret searches in intelligence investigations, including international terrorism cases; before 1994, the Attorney General authorized secret searches in intelligence investigations of terrorist groups without any judicial scrutiny. And during the limited debate over the PATRIOT Act, reasonable voices proposed that secret searches be statutorily authorized in criminal investigations of terrorism.

As enacted, however, section 213 was not limited to terrorism cases. It would astound most Americans that government agents could enter their homes while they are asleep or their places of business while they are away and carry out a secret search or seizure and not tell them until weeks or months later. It would especially astound them that this authority is available for all federal offenses, ranging from weapons of mass destruction investigations to student loan cases. That is what section 213 of the PATRIOT Act authorizes. Indeed, the Justice Department has admitted that it has used section 213 sneak-and-peek authority in nonviolent cases having nothing to do with terrorism. These include, according to the Justice Department's October 24, 2003 letter to Senator Stevens, an investigation of judicial corruption, where agents carried out a sneak-and-peek search of a judge's chambers, a fraudulent checks case, and a health care fraud investigation, which involved a sneak-and-peek of a home nursing care business.

Section 213 fails in its stated purpose of establishing a uniform statutory standard applicable to sneak-and-peek searches throughout the United States. For a number of years, under various standards, courts had allowed delayed notice or sneak-and-peek searches. The term "sneak and peek," by the way, was not contrived by opponents of the PATRIOT Act—before the PATRIOT Act, it was used by FBI agents, DOJ officials, and judicial opinions. Rather than "codifying existing case law under a single national standard to streamline detective work," section 213 confuses the law. Rather than trying to devise a standard suitable to breaking and entering into homes and offices for delayed notice searches, Congress in the haste of the PATRIOT Act merely incorporated by reference a definition of "adverse result" adopted in 1986 for completely unrelated purposes, concerning access to e-mail stored on the computer of an ISP. Under that standard, secret searches of homes and offices can be allowed not only in cases that could result in endangering the life of a person or destruction of evidence, but also in any case that might involve "intimidation of potential witnesses" or "seriously jeopardizing an investigation" or "unduly delaying a trial." These broad concepts offer little guidance to judges and will bring about no national uniformity in sneak-and-peek cases.

Section 213 also leaves judges guessing as to how long notice may be delayed. The Second and Ninth Circuits had adopted, as a basic presumption, a seven-day rule for the initial delay. Section 213 says that notice may be delayed for "a reasonable period." Does this mean that lower courts in the Ninth Circuit and the Second Circuit no longer have to adhere to the seven-day rule? At the least, it suggests that courts outside those Circuits could make up their own rules. "Reasonable period" affords judges considering sneak-and-peek searches no uniform standard.

If, as section 213 supporters claim, sneak-and-peek searches are a "time-honored tool," and if courts "around the country have been issuing them for decades," as DOJ claims, why did the Justice Department push so hard in the PATRIOT Act for a section 213 applicable to all cases? The answer, I believe, is that the sneak-and-peek concept stands on shaky constitutional ground, and the Justice Department was trying to bolster it with congressional action—even action by a Congress that thought it was voting on an anti-terrorism bill, not a general crimes bill.

The fact is, there is a constitutional problem with section 213: the sneak-and-peek cases rest on an interpretation of the Fourth Amendment that is no longer valid. The major Circuit Court opinions allowing sneak-and-peek searches date from the 1986, *United States v. Freitas*, 800 F.2d 1451 (9th Cir.), and 1990, *United States v. Villegas*, 899 F.2d 1324 (2d Cir.). These cases were premised on the assumption that notice was not an element of the Fourth Amendment. *United States v. Pangburn*, 983 F.2d 449, 453 (2d Cir. 1993) starts its discussion of sneak-and-peek searches by stating: "No provision specifically requiring notice of the execution of a search warrant is included in the Fourth Amendment." *Pangburn* goes on to state, "The Fourth Amendment does not deal with notice of any kind. . . ."

Yet in *Wilson v. Arkansas*, 514 U.S. 927 (1995), in a unanimous opinion by Justice Thomas, the Supreme Court held that the knock and notice requirement of common law was incorporated in the Fourth Amendment as part of the constitutional inquiry into reasonableness. Notice is part of the Fourth Amendment, the court held, directly repudiating the premise of the sneak-and-peek cases. *Wilson v. Arkansas* makes it clear that a search without notice is not always unreasonable, but surely the case requires a different analysis of the issue than was given it by those courts that assumed that notice was not a part of the constitutional framework for searches at all. A much more carefully crafted set of standards for sneak-and-peek searches, including both stricter limits of the circumstances under which they can be approved and a seven-day time limit, is called for.

Section 213's attempted codification of the sneak-and-peek authority went too far. To fix it, Congress should leave the statutory authority in place but add several limitations:

- Section 213 only requires a judge to find "reasonable cause" to believe that an adverse result will happen if notice is not delayed. "Reasonable cause" doesn't even mean that the harmful result is likely. For such a momentous decision, "probable cause" to believe would be a more appropriate standard.
- Congress should narrow the circumstances in which notification may be delayed so that section 213 does not apply to virtually every search. Under section 213, the government need only show that providing notice would seriously jeopar-

dize an investigation or unduly delay a trial. This "catch-all" standard could apply in almost every case and therefore is simply too broad for this uniquely intrusive type of search. Congress should allow sneak-and-peek searches only if giving notice would likely result in danger to the life or physical safety of an individual, flight from prosecution, destruction of or tampering with evidence, or intimidation of potential witnesses.

- Congress should require that any delay in notification not extend for more than seven days without additional judicial authorization. Section 213 permits delay for a "reasonable time" period, which is undefined in the statute. Pre-PATRIOT Act case law in the Ninth and Second Circuits stated that seven days was an appropriate time period. Indeed, DOJ's internal guidance recognizes that seven days is the most common period, but also suggests that it may seek much longer delays. Congress should set a basic seven-day rule, while permitting the Justice Department to obtain additional seven-day extensions of the delay if it can continue to meet one of the requirements for authorizing delay in the first instance.

- Finally, Congress should require the Justice Department to report on its use of the sneak-and-peek power. The Attorney General should report the number of requests for delayed notification, the number of those requests granted or denied, and the number of extensions requested, granted, and denied, so that Congress and the public can determine if this technique is being narrowly applied.

Even with these changes, sneak-and-peek searches, especially of homes, stand on shaky constitutional ground except in investigations of the most serious crimes. Judicial caution is necessary. The reasonable changes outlined above would leave the statutory authority in place but bring it under more appropriate limitations and oversight, affording law enforcement a useful tool in extraordinary cases but preserving the constitutional norm reflected in both Supreme Court decisions and popular TV dramas: "Police! Open the door. We have a warrant."

Heather Mac Donald

Response

Mr. Dempsey's response conforms flawlessly to the anti-PATRIOT act template. He relies on the two central tropes: Conceal Legal Precedent and Hide the Judge.

Mr. Dempsey implies that section 213 is a radical new power: "It would astound most Americans that government agents could enter their homes while they are asleep or their places of business while they are away and carry out a secret search or seizure and not tell them until weeks or months later. . . . That is what section 213 of the PATRIOT Act authorizes." No, that is what federal judges have authorized for decades; section 213 merely codifies those precedents. If such a law enforcement power is "astounding," Mr. Dempsey should have challenged those precedents long ago. And this delayed notice capacity might appear less "astounding" if Mr. Dempsey acknowledged as an initial matter that agents can delay notice only after convincing a judge that notice would have an "adverse result," such as harm to an individual or witness intimidation.

It is irrelevant that section 213 is not confined to terrorism investigations; neither were the precedents that it codified.

Mr. Dempsey's efforts to find "confusion" in the section's language are unconvincing. Such terms as "intimidation of potential witnesses" or "seriously jeopardizing an investigation" are no more confusing than any other statutory or constitutional mandate. All statutes require judges to fit legislative language to the facts of a case; if no interpretation were necessary, we could use computers to rule on disputes.

It is perfectly appropriate that section 213 allows judges discretion as to what a "reasonable period" for delay is. Mr. Dempsey worries that this discretion will allow judges to "make up their own rules." Welcome to the common law! Congress rightly decided that it lacked the foresight to predict in every case how long a witness's life might be at risk, say, from a search target.

110

Wilson v. Arkansas, 514 U.S. 927 (1995), poses no threat to delayed notice authority. The Court emphasized that the "Fourth Amendment's flexible requirement of reasonableness should not be read to mandate a rigid rule of announcement that ignores countervailing law enforcement interests." Those interests include situations, the Court said, "where police officers have reason to believe that evidence would likely be destroyed if advance notice were given."

Mr. Dempsey claims that Wilson now requires a probable cause standard for the judicial finding of "adverse result." The Court has already rejected that argument in *Richards v. Wisconsin*, 520 U.S. 385 (1997), however. The "reasonable suspicion . . . standard—as opposed to a probable cause requirement—strikes the appropriate balance between the legitimate law enforcement concerns at issue in the execution of search warrants and the individual privacy interests affected by no-knock entries," the Court said.

The grounds for delaying notice are appropriate and need not be amended. Mr. Dempsey thinks that "seriously jeopardizing" an investigation is not a valid reason to delay notice. This position offends common sense and is contrary to the law. *United States v. John*, 508 F.2d 1134 (8th Cir. 1975); *cert. denied*, 421 U.S. 962 (1975), found that ensuring the continued effectiveness of a criminal investigation satisfied the "good cause" requirement for delaying notice of a Title III wiretap under 18 U.S.C. section 2518(d).

In conclusion, section 213 does not "expand government powers," as Mr. Dempsey claims; nor does it lack "suitable checks and balances"—judicial review is the cornerstone of the section. Delayed notice is an imperative power for terrorism investigations, as well as for other criminal investigations where notice may imperil persons or the pursuit of justice.

James X. Dempsey

The Last Word

It is clear that the PATRIOT Act standard is simply too liberal. As the prior essay points out, in the first 19 months under the current section 213 standard, no judge ever denied a government sneak-and-peek request. Far from wanting to "hide the judge," supporters of a more balanced approach want to give judges clearer authority to approve secret searches when necessary while ensuring that the exception does not swallow the rule.

Supreme Court decisions in *Wilson v. Arkansas* and *Richards v. Wisconsin* make it clear that the constitutional rule is prior notice of searches, through knock and announce. The Court allowed an exception to this rule, upon "reasonable suspicion," by allowing police to provide notice as they were entering when they faced a life-threatening situation or the destruction of evidence. Notice in Wilson and Richards was immediate; it just wasn't given in advance. If "reasonable suspicion" is the standard for delaying notice by minutes, probable cause should be the standard when notice is delayed for days or weeks.

As noted, the Justice Department has reported to Congress on its use of section 213. Codifying this practice would allow Congress and the public to assess in years to come if the standard is too strict or too liberal. The fact that a defender of the PATRIOT Act would oppose routine reporting on how it is working shows the unreasonableness of the "don't change a comma" position.

Borders

George J. Terwilliger III
Timothy Edgar

Controlling the Border: A Matter of Safety, Sovereignty, and Fairness

George J. Terwilliger III

Introduction

The relative ease with which irregular combatants can enter United States territory to attack civilian and military targets is an obvious and present threat to our national security. In addition to the potential for thousands of casualties, attacks by these intruders could cripple our economic infrastructure. Moreover, successful attacks would call into question the very ability of our government to perform its most fundamental responsibility: defending the homeland and its inhabitants.

In addition, the failure to control our borders and immigration generally results in manifest unfairness to immigrants and visitors alike, disrespect for the rule of law, and a great disservice to our own citizens, who rightfully expect the government to guard the nation's frontiers effectively.

A nation that cannot or does not control its borders fails in "a fundamental act of sovereignty." *United States ex rel. Knauff v. Shaughnessy*, 338 U.S. 537, 542 (1950). It is past time for the United States to reassert this sovereignty. The September 11 Commission found the vulnerability arising from the chaotic state of immigration law and enforcement to be among the pressing concerns requiring prompt attention. *See* National Commission on Terrorist

Attacks on the United States, *The 9/11 Commission Report*, at 387-90. Under the current legal and enforcement regime, the population of persons illegally in the United States is estimated to have reached nine million and climbing. *See* Ruth Ellen Wasem, *Unauthorized Aliens in the United States: Estimates Since 1986*, CRS Report RS21938 (2004). Meanwhile, many foreign nationals—students, businesspeople, tourists, and others—wait patiently abroad to enter in a lawful manner for a lawful reason.

Yet while the threat, and the need for reform, are relatively clear, the commitment to control our borders as part of a comprehensive defense has not materialized. The stepped-up enforcement of immigration laws and reordering of intelligence-related assets that have occurred are very positive developments, but are not enough. In the past, terrorists have employed almost every means available to enter or remain in the United States—student and tourist visas, asylum applications, false passports, and many others. Without a reassertion of control over the border, including broad immigration law reforms, we will remain fundamentally as vulnerable in this respect as we were on September 10, 2001.

The Legal Authority for Immigration Control

The legal authority necessary to reassert sovereignty over the border is readily available. The national government has plenary authority to control who enters the United States and under what circumstances and conditions. *Knauff*, 338 U.S. at 542. The exercise of this power is committed to the political branches. Congressional power in this regard is apparent from the combined import of the Commerce Clause, the Naturalization Clause, and the Necessary and Proper Clause of the Constitution. The executive power to exclude aliens "is inherent in the executive power to control the foreign affairs of the nation." *Id.* The judicial branch has only limited authority to review the execution of relevant laws for due process concerns. *Id.* at 543 ("it is not within the province of any court, unless expressly authorized by law, to review the determination of the political branch of government to exclude a given alien").

Steps to Reasserting Sovereignty Over the Borders

Physical Control of the Borders. Several steps should be considered as means to reassert sovereignty over our borders. First, we must regain effective physical control of the borders. At least 300,000 people enter the country illegally without inspection each year. Chicago Council on Foreign Relations, *Keeping the Promise: Immigration Proposals from the Heartland* at 28 (2004). It is time to stop pursuing the fiction that simply adding more border officers will curb illegal entries. The borders should be temporarily hardened with physical barriers that can be manned and patrolled effectively. The proposed national security fence along the border with Mexico would be a large step in the right direction. No less is required on the northern border. That open frontier has been used for decades by all manner of underworld elements to evade immigration control, including bootleggers in the 1920s, heroin smugglers in the 1970s, and terrorists in recent years. The first known attempt by a Middle Eastern terrorist group to bring an explosive device into the United States occurred on the Vermont-Quebec border in 1986. Today, Montreal in the East, and Vancouver in the West, are major first stops for aliens and contraband coming to North America from overseas.

Any border fence must have a wide metaphorical gate, open to those who would legitimately come here to see or pursue the American dream. The borders must, however, be closed to those who would bring contraband, terrorist violence, or weapons of mass destruction into the country.

National Identity Card System. In addition, an effective national identity card system, utilizing biometric identifying information, should be implemented. A national identity card system could not only provide the foundation for effective immigration control, it could also combat identity theft; criminals are a greater threat to privacy in the information age than the government. The program must have stringent privacy protections, including built-in restrictions on access to the data connected with it. Strict criminal sanctions should also be created for illegal use of the card or system data.

Reforms to Immigration Laws

A number of reforms to immigration laws now on the books are called for as well. First, an amnesty program along the lines recently discussed would be sensible. It is not a good use of resources to seek the apprehension and exclusion of law-abiding aliens who entered through the gaping holes in our system and are now making positive social and economic contributions. For would-be entrants from abroad, special, enhanced inspection procedures, and potentially an immigration freeze, could be initiated for persons meeting a special screening profile that includes ethnicity and nationality among the criteria utilized. Treating all alien applicants for entry as equal threats to security, as our system now does, is both wasteful of precious resources and dangerously unrealistic. Such a system fails to focus on criteria drawn from reliable data that would allow more efficiency, greater effectiveness, and real fairness in distinguishing between legitimate applicants and security threats. An immigration system that fails to use available knowledge to discriminate among all applicants to identify the more likely threats is no system at all. It is unfair to the majority of law-abiding people and subjects our efforts to scorn and ridicule. Such monuments to mindless political correctness need to be dismantled.

Further, the practice of paroling asylum applicants and other would-be emigres into the United States pending decision on their applications should be ended except in rare, specific cases (e.g., children paroled into the custody of relatives in the United States). Under the current system, an applicant may be temporarily admitted to the United States and released until the date of the hearing on his application. Unsurprisingly, a substantial percentage of those thus paroled do not return for the hearings on their applications. This system could be replaced with one under which all applications would have to be made and decided upon at a United States embassy or consulate overseas. Aliens who arrive at United States borders requesting asylum could be returned to their point of embarkation, or if such return would pose an undue risk to them, to a third country, and either held or released there pending application for asylum at a United States embassy or consulate. In the few cases in which that is impossible, detention here should be mandatory pending review of the application at an embassy or consulate in the country of embarkation.

Finally, as to those found violating immigration laws in the future, any person administratively determined to have entered or attempted to enter the United States unlawfully should be permanently excluded, without the right to judicial review. If such a person were later found in the United States, a period of incarceration of up to five years, and/or deportation at any time without judicial review, would be appropriate. Similarly, any application to enter or remain in United States that is administratively determined to be false or fraudulent should result in the forfeiture of any rights the applicant may have to be in the United States.

Complete and Compatible Fingerprint Identification System

Lastly, all persons applying to visit, immigrate, or apprehended having entered or trying to enter United States illegally should be ten-print fingerprinted electronically and assigned a number that should be permanent. The method of fingerprinting used by the Department of Homeland Security must be compatible with that used by the FBI, so that the fingerprints of aliens encountered by DHS officials may be cross-referenced to those in the FBI's database. The incompatibility between the databases used by these authorities—identified, among other sources, in a March 2004 report by the Inspector General of the Department of Justice—cannot be allowed to persist.

Conclusion

For both its national security interests and in vindication of the rule of law, the United States needs to reassert immediately its sovereign right to control its borders. We must be prepared to accept that many, including friends abroad, will object vehemently to any reforms that tighten restrictions on aliens' access to the United States. We must also, of course, undertake these changes without diminishing our historic welcome to lawful immigrants and visitors. Indeed, these reforms must be undertaken not only for the sake of national security, but also to provide fairness to those who would come lawfully in the footsteps of the thousands, including one of my grandfathers, who came before them and from whose labors the nation we know today was built.

Timothy Edgar

Conceding the Battle: Heavy-Handed Immigration Measures
Three Years After 9/11

The still-potent memory of the terrorist attacks of September 11, 2001, continues to spur forward proposals that will diminish our nation's respect for the fundamental freedoms of aspiring immigrants and noncitizens as well as citizens of the United States. Perhaps the greatest flaw in most of the "reform" proposals pushed under the banner of national security, moreover, is that they will do nothing to enhance our safety. Indeed, for the most part, these proposals are simply unworkable, pre-9/11 schemes advanced by anti-immigration advocates who quite literally favor putting a wall around America. Put simply, we need not lock down our borders or abrogate our fundamental freedoms to stop terrorists. Indeed, if we do take the wrong fork in the road, we will have all but conceded the ideological battle with our enemies.

While the crowning jewel of the anti-immigration proposals has always been a Berlin Wall–style barrier along the Southwest border with Mexico (now, amazingly, proposed to be extended along 4,000 miles of Canadian border as well), this proposal simply fails under its own weight whenever seriously proposed. Put plainly, those dollars would be better spent to bring the intelligence community's information technology into the 21st century, to train and hire translators and analysts to comb through the backlog of intelligence intercepts, and to update the immigration service's notoriously inaccurate record-keeping system.

In the main, the anti-immigration proposals with the strongest support of the anti-immigrant lobby in Congress involve diminishing the rights of the vulnerable, rather than spending the resources needed on effective border security. In the fall of 2004, House Judiciary Chairman F. James Sensenbrenner, R-WI, held hostage intelligence reform legislation endorsed by the National Commission on Terrorist Attacks upon the United States, or 9/11 Commission, insisting on a package of misguided anti-immigration provisions. These were proposals the 9/11 Commission had specifically refrained from endorsing after careful study. While Sensenbrenner failed to garner support for the more extreme immigration provisions, he has managed to ram these proposals through the House again early this year in the form of a bill styled the "REAL I.D. Act" by supporters.

The REAL I.D. Act includes:

- a waiver of "all laws" to expedite construction of a border fence;
- changes to the asylum process that make it more difficult for claimants to find haven in the United States;
- legislation to limit when immigrants ordered deported or detained can seek habeas corpus relief in the federal courts;
- retroactive application of new grounds for removal;
- and, last but certainly not least, a national identification system keyed to immigration status in the guise of new rules for our now-federalized driver's licenses.

This last, of course, poses additional considerations for both privacy rights and sound principles of federalism (in that even a moderately secure system would be inordinately costly to implement, with the lion's share of such costs passed onto the states through new, unfunded mandates on the state motor vehicles bureaus). Though one can certainly appreciate the need to intercept terrorists and other threats before they can enter the country, these proposals are not calculated to meet that challenge and would result in extensive collateral damage were they to be adopted.

If passed, the REAL I.D. Act would make the driver's license provisions in the intelligence reform bill far more invasive, requiring states to link their motor vehicle licensing databases with those of Canada, Mexico, and the other states, and would force states to integrate immigration status information into their licensing infrastructures. This latter requirement would apply even if it were at odds with state statutes. Practically, this unfunded mandate would impress state Department of Motor Vehicle employees into service as untrained, ill-equipped deputies of federal immigration authorities. Notably, this commandeering of state resources for immigration enforcement is the same approach in the Clear Law Enforcement for Criminal Alien Removal (CLEAR) Act, H.R. 2162, 108th Cong. (2004), which died in committee but would have required local and state law enforcement officials to enforce federal immigration laws.

The most pressing unanswered question is how this change would help intercept terrorists before they strike. The majority of the hijackers were in the country under valid, unexpired visas, and all traveled under their own names. Even counterfeit-resistant, biometric identification can only be as good as the documents (such as a birth certificate) on which it is based. The security of birth certificates can be enhanced, of course, but any changes made now will have little effect for decades. Imposing federal mandates on state driver's licenses to catch undocumented workers, under the facade of counterterrorism, will provide only false security. The local DMV will try and fail to round up undocumented workers, and local police will instead notice an increase in unlicensed, uninsured drivers on the highways who are reluctant to help them catch criminals. Meanwhile, actual terrorists will be able use counterfeit precursor documents to obtain valid identification, which, because of a false sense of security, will be unquestioned everywhere in the country.

The Sensenbrenner bill also goes after one of the most vulnerable populations: those fleeing persecution from countries like China, North Korea, and Iran. Asylum applicants are already among the most scrutinized of noncitizens to enter the country—all are fingerprinted and given extensive background checks. According to the 9/11 Commission, this is a major reason Al Qaeda turned to business visas, not asylum applications, to mount the 9/11 attack. The 9/11 Commission did not recommend making it more difficult to obtain asylum and criticized the use of immigration laws to round up innocent Arab and Muslim noncitizens.

The REAL I.D. Act ignores these findings, making it more difficult for claimants to find haven in the United States. Specifically, the bill would permit federal officials to require "corroboration," such as police reports or other documents, for what would be otherwise valid claims of persecution or torture. This would have the sublime effect of, for instance, putting the fate of those escaping the Janjaweed militias in Darfur in the hands of their sponsors in Khartoum who have control of the official documents that are demanded. The bill then limits the ability of the federal courts to reverse denials of asylum claims on that basis.

Incoming Secretary of Homeland Security Michael Chertoff criticized just such a corroboration requirement while on the federal bench. In *Chen v. Attorney General*, 81 Fed. App. 418, No. 0002-4303 (Nov. 23, 2003), the Third Circuit upheld the denial of asylum for a Chinese woman who claimed she was forced to undergo forced abortion and sterilization. Chertoff's vigorous dissent pilloried the requirement, imposed by an overzealous immigration official, that the woman produce a government certificate verifying the date of the abortion. "Chen submitted a State Department report stating that Chinese authorities do not issue abortion certificates for involuntary abortions," he wrote. "If so, that would seem a pretty persuasive reason why no such certificate could be provided to corroborate an involuntary abortion." *Id.* at 425 (Chertoff, J., dissenting). The REAL I.D. Act would, however, insulate just such arbitrary decisions from judicial review.

Finally, the REAL I.D. bill seeks to amend the 2001 USA PATRIOT Act, Pub. L. 107-056, 115 Stat. 272, 107th Cong. (2001), to enable the government to deport long-term, lawful permanent residents for providing humanitarian support to groups that immigration authorities later assert fit the definition of a "terrorist group." The provision would require the deportation of the noncitizen even if the support was completely lawful at the time it was provided. Support, even humanitarian support, for a designated terrorist group is, of course, already grounds for deportation, not to mention a serious felony. The Sensenbrenner bill, however, would make lawful donations made even decades ago by permanent residents who have lived in America for many years retroactive grounds for deportation, even if the recipient organization has never been added to an official government terrorist list. Though the PATRIOT Act makes such support grounds for refusing a potential immigrant admission to the country, to have it become a retroactive tool for the summary deportation of lawful and law-abiding permanent residents seems vindictive and unnecessary.

The REAL I.D. Act is only a taste of a much broader anti-immigrant agenda, which continues to advance even three years after 9/11. Some even argue, for instance, that law enforcement should openly structure investigative and security-screening tactics around immutable group characteristics like race, religion or ethnicity. This proposal ignores the experiences in Chechnya and Israel, where terrorists have used women or teenagers to successfully foil security "profiles" (not to mention deep-seated American ideals of equality under the law and basic fairness). America itself saw the folly of profiling at work during the Oklahoma City bombing investigation, which spurred an immediate manhunt for Middle Eastern terrorists, with the perpetrator turning out to be homegrown. While opponents of racial and ethnic profiling are often scorned as "politically correct," it is police chiefs themselves, like the police chief who headed the Washington, D.C.-area sniper investigation, who have protested most loudly against this ineffective and counterproductive tactic.

Demands for the United States to diminish basic, fundamental freedoms to secure American borders and sovereignty are dangerously misguided and obscure the real issues in border security. The only way to stop terrorists—or anyone else—from entering the country is to spend adequate resources, through a reformed intelligence system, to identify terrorist suspects and arrest them when they attempt to enter the country. Federal attention must be focused on this extremely difficult task, not on a nativist agenda masquerading as counterterrorism policy.

George J. Terwilliger III

Response

We are engaged not, as the response would have it, in an "ideological battle with our enemies," but in a real war in which those enemies seek to continue to kill Americans. The relevant ideological battle in the context of control of the nation's borders is between those who believe that the rule of law means that everyone has to obey the law and those who believe that an ineffective and outdated system may be left in place, even in the face of a grave threat to national security.

There is nothing "anti-immigrant" or "anti-immigration" about the initial essay. Indeed, the points and proposals raised therein are pro-immigration. Immigration is a strong fiber in the fabric of our society, but a certain path to pulling that thread loose is continuing to ignore gaping holes in our immigration law and procedures, continuing to reward those who first come to the United States by committing illegal acts and turning a blind eye to the patently obvious security risks that current immigration and border enforcement engenders. The approach advocated by the response—apparently to permit the status quo to persist—would ignore serious security issues, reward lawbreakers, and send a message to the thousands who patiently wait to emigrate to the U.S. through lawful means that their compliance with the law only leaves them waiting at the border while their places are taken by those who cheat to enter the country.

The original essay did not advocate wholesale adoption of the provisions of the REAL I.D. Act. Nevertheless, certain aspects of that act (or slightly modified versions of the measures called for therein) could provide real benefits both in making our system of immigration law more efficient and effective and in the war on terrorism. A national I.D. card containing biometric identifying data linked to an integrated database, for instance, would enhance security and ease enforcement of existing immigration laws. The primary objections to such a proposal raised in the response appear to be that such an I.D. would be easy to obtain using counterfeit precursor documents and that such a system would impose an undue burden on the states through unfunded mandates. These arguments are essentially red herrings. Far from creating a false sense of security, a card containing biometric information would require precisely the kind of point of contact with government authorities that terrorists seeking to conceal their true identities seek to avoid. Moreover, such a system need not be implemented through unfunded mandates.

Similarly, the reforms to asylum procedures suggested in the initial essay are not dealt with in the response, which instead focuses on the REAL I.D. Act's proposal to permit a corroboration requirement as part of that process. Regardless of the wisdom of imposing a corroboration requirement, it is simply not the case that, as the response suggests, asylum applicants are so carefully scrutinized as to render it unlikely that terrorists will use this avenue to enter the country. Indeed, Ramzi Yousef, architect of the first World Trade Center bombing, entered the country as a paroled asylum applicant.

I should note that I agree with the response insofar as it suggests that the most important weapon in the counterterrorism arsenal is intelligence. As I noted in testimony to the Senate Judiciary Committee in April 2002, knowledge is the most important weapon we have in the war against terrorists. We cannot remain a free society without remaining vulnerable at some level to those willing to subvert the rule of law and surrender their own lives in order to create mayhem and destruction. The only way to best such people is to know who they are and what they are planning, and to stop them. Reforming our approach to control of the borders is but one prong in what must be a multifaceted strategy to combat the threat of terrorism.

Timothy Edgar

___

The Last Word

I could not agree more with the rebuttal that the ultimate purpose of our system of laws is their equitable application. The problem, however, with many of the policies proposed in a "Fortress America" approach is that they would, in the name of enforcing the law, require the government to violate that most basic of all laws: the Constitution. As Brandeis said, "Our government is the potent, the omnipresent teacher. For good or ill, it teaches the whole people by its example."

The best example of this constitutional problem is the proposed requirement that asylum seekers provide corroboration from their home government of either past or future persecution. As the government that would be doing the corroborating is also often the persecutor, this policy effectively treats asylum claimants as unworthy of the same due process the Fifth Amendment provides to all persons, not merely citizens. This is not closing a "loophole," it is making it more difficult than it was before for asylum claimants to put forward a successful claim.

To be clear, we do not seek to excuse wrongdoers from answering to the law. But the approach of the rebuttal is simply more of the same—more court-stripping, more government forms, more walls and fences. America has been following this approach since the 1996 immigration laws, without success in preventing illegal immigration or the entry of terrorists. If we keep it, the authorities could easily miss Mohammed Atta walking down the concourse with a fake ID, while they spend their time and resources on the deportation of a yet another hard-working young man from Mexico City.

Detainees

Patricia Wald and Joe Onek
John Yoo and Gregory Jacob

Go Slow on Expanding Detention Authority

Patricia Wald and Joe Onek

T he right to be free from arbitrary restraint of one's physical freedom has traditionally been considered a bulwark liberty guaranteed by our Constitution. Justice O'Connor last year described it as "the most elemental of liberty interests—the interest in being free from physical detention by one's own government," an interest as strong in war as in peace (*Hamdi v. Rumsfeld*). In ordinary times, for U.S. citizens and legal aliens, that interest is invaded primarily through the invocation of the criminal law processes, involving arrests on probable cause of law violation and arraignment with a right to counsel before a magistrate who must find that the person presents a risk of flight or danger to another person or the community before he can be detained pending the outcome of the criminal trial or appeal (18 U.S.C. 1342). The criminal law also permits judges to detain a U.S. person as a material witness if his presence at criminal proceedings cannot otherwise be assured (18 U.S.C. 1344). In the case of noncitizens subject to deportation, a judge may order detention pending deportation if they pose a flight risk or danger to the community. These simple rules have provided the basic legal framework for detentions within the United States. Experimentation with mass detentions of U.S. citizens and foreign-born residents outside the criminal and deportation regimes, such as the infamous internments of the 120,000 loyal Japanese-Americans, have been universally (albeit retrospectively) condemned, producing statutory bans against their feared repetition (18 U.S.C. 4001).

After 9/11 things changed rapidly. In the weeks following the attacks, more than 1,200 American citizens and aliens were detained and imprisoned outside the limits of the ordinary criminal law procedures or the Immigration Act. The government refused to make known the identities or whereabouts of any of these detainees at first and later provided such information only about those charged with criminal violations (a small minority).

These mass detentions were justified as necessary to investigate and prevent "threats, conspiracies, and attempts to perpetrate terrorist acts against the United States."

The criminal charges eventually brought against a limited number (approximately 130) were predominantly for minor charges, which would not justify detention under the usual criteria for pretrial release, and very few detainees were ever charged with a terrorist act.

As to the detainees held on (often technical) immigration violations, pre-hearing release decisions by immigration judges were barred and many detainees were denied access to counsel or family for weeks or months. In addition, the dockets and hearings were kept strictly secret. Although there may have been technical legal bases for many of the post-9/11 arrests—minor criminal charges and immigration violations—the pool of those questioned was determined largely by "tips" from less than reliable sources and speculation based on racial and ethnic origins. Some detainees suffered abuse by guards while in prison (Report of the Office of the Inspector General, Department of Justice).

The preventive detention of aliens went far beyond anything authorized by Congress. In the PATRIOT Act, Congress amended the Immigration and Nationality Act to authorize the Attorney General or his designee to certify that an alien was engaged in activity that endangered the security of the United States and to detain such alien for seven days before bringing immigration or criminal charges (PATRIOT Act, § 412).

This provision was never used; the government was able to detain aliens without charges for far longer periods by simply imprisoning them secretly and denying them access to hearings or counsel.

A small subset of detainees, both citizens and aliens, were held under the criminal law as material witnesses. The federal material witness statute permits the government, under limited circumstances, to detain persons who are required as witnesses in future judicial proceedings and who cannot be relied upon to appear at those proceedings. But after 9/11, people were held as material witnesses even though the government acknowledged that "it may turn out these individuals have no information useful to the government," and even though it has been reported that almost half of them never testified before a grand jury (*Washington Post*, Nov. 24, 2002 at A1).

The last category of persons detained post-9/11 in the United States outside of the traditional legal framework involves a few persons (two citizens and one alien) designated as "enemy combatants" by the President and held by the military without access to lawyers or any outside contacts. The articulated basis for these detentions is the "law of war," which allows one State at war with another to detain any of the combatants fighting for the enemy as long as active combat exists. The extension of this customary law to the situation of a U.S. citizen detained in this country who was not an enemy soldier or had not been captured on the battlefield has never been sanctioned by our courts or by international law or practice.

Jose Padilla, an American citizen seized at O'Hare Airport and held first as a material witness, later transferred to enemy combatant status and detained incommunicado in a military brig, had his petition for habeas corpus dismissed by the Supreme Court because it was brought in an inappropriate district. However, in the *Padilla* and *Hamdi* cases, five justices signaled that they would not approve the protracted incommunicado detention of an American citizen. At the very least, the *Hamdi* case appears to ensure that a citizen detained as an enemy combatant will be entitled to a hearing before an impartial tribunal and notice of charges, as well as the right to confront evidence against him and presumably to counsel. Only one noncitizen (Ali al-Marri) has been detained in the U.S. as an enemy combatant, and his habeas proceeding is still at an early stage.

This, then, is the state of domestic detention practices in the post-9/11 world—as far as we know it. It raises intriguing and troublesome questions, among which are: Does our experience with post-9/11 terrorism threats so far suggest that within the United States, traditional law enforcement and deportation powers are not sufficient? The proponents of expanded detention powers raise worst-case scenarios—as far as we can tell, all hypothetical, yet not totally implausible. We examine one such hypothetical case. A suspect (either a citizen or legal alien) is picked up in the United States on the basis of strong, credible evidence that he is planning a terrorist attack in the near future. The source of the evidence would, if disclosed at trial, seriously compromise an ongoing intelligence effort to monitor actions of high-level Al Qaeda leaders. If the suspect is given access to counsel, he will almost certainly be advised (at least at the outset) not to cooperate because of the many extant legal issues concerning the legitimacy of his arrest and detention. Do we need a new detention power to deal with this situation?

In this hypothetical, it is difficult to imagine that a magistrate would not find reason to hold the suspect on probable cause of a criminal offense and detain him pending trial. The magistrate would also be able to close all pretrial hearings if necessary to protect classified national security information. Extension of the trial date might well fit the waiver provision of the Speedy Trial Act (18 U.S.C. § (8)(A)), and if not, a modest legislative amendment would accomplish the result. The only real gap left in current law would be the government's interest in uncounselled interrogation, an interest not heretofore recognized as a legitimate goal of detention.

Heymann and Kayyem (*see* Philip B. Heymann and Julliette N. Kayyem, *Preserving Security and Democratic Freedoms in the War on Terrorism* (2004)) have proposed more extensive revisions to current law. They would retain the general rule that U.S. citizens seized within our borders be adjudicated for acts of terrorism (or the planning thereof) under our criminal law—expanded if necessary to cover all such activities. Suspects might be detained by a magistrate under the regular detention law on a showing that no other means is available to insure against their risk to the community. If information of a national security nature is involved in making such a showing, a specially appointed defense counsel or advocate who has been cleared can participate in the closed hearing. A period of seven days for interrogation without access to counsel could also be approved by the judge upon an additional showing that it was reasonably believed to be necessary to prevent a terrorist act. If a trial is not feasible even under the Classified Information Procedures Act because of national security reasons, delay may be authorized up to two years, after which the suspect must be tried or released. A person who is not a U.S. citizen or resident alien could be seized on the basis of affidavits that he is planning or about to engage in a terrorist act and held for 48 hours before he is taken to a judge, who may order detention in periodic installments up to two years on clear and convincing evidence he is participating in terrorist activities. He may be refused access to counsel if the government demonstrates to the judge that counsel will prevent a lawful interrogation from being successful— as to which showing a "special advocate" for the defense may see the evidence and make a case for its insufficiency.

Such a regime would face criticism from both national security advocates and civil libertarians. For the former, it rejects their fundamental premise that the power to detain enemies in the U.S. during wartime (including a war on terror) is one constitutionally entrusted to the President and, by his delegation, to the military. They will particularly object to giving suspects any access to counsel, arguing that this will interfere with interrogations. Civil libertarians, on the other hand, citing Justice Scalia's opinion in *Hamdi*, will contend that Congress is constitutionally without power to deprive domestic detainees of the procedural safeguards of the Fifth and Sixth Amendments except under the highly limited circumstances warranting suspension of the writ of habeas corpus. They will argue that existing criminal and immigration procedures are adequate to protect national security and will object to delays in the provision of counsel and commencement of trial and to the special rules for noncitizens.

Congress may well consider preventive detention legislation in this session, particularly if the courts rule against the government's assertion of unlimited power to detain in the pending enemy combatant cases. But before expanding the government's power, Congress should study and remedy the misuse of existing powers that occurred after 9/11. Although one might take heart from the relatively prompt and effective exposure by the DOJ Inspector General of the abuses in the roundup of immigrants and the subsequent assurances from government officials that certain of these abuses would not happen again, Congress should consider legislation appropriately restricting secret arrests, detention without charges, and closed deportation hearings. Similarly, Congress should consider legislation to prevent the use of the material witness statute as a holding device when no testimony is contemplated. With respect to preventive detention legislation, Congress should not take hurried action. We have seen in the case of noncitizens held outside the U.S. that prolonged incommunicado detention without access to courts, counsel or family invites widespread abuse and even torture. This bitter experience should give Congress and the American people pause in creating a new detention regime in the U.S., even if that regime is in civilian and judicial hands. At this juncture, the need for such a new regime has not been demonstrated, and Americans should be cautious and watchful before radically changing our system of justice to meet a hypothetical danger.

John Yoo and Gregory Jacob

The Power to Detain Enemy Combatants in War

Critics of the Bush Administration's treatment of enemy combatants captured during the War on Terror raise two primary objections. First, some critics contend that the President lacks authority under the Constitution and the laws of war to detain enemy combatants, particularly enemy combatants who happen to be U.S. citizens or are captured on U.S. soil. If enemy combatants are to be held long-term, these critics argue, the executive branch must resort to traditional criminal processes, beginning with the bringing of criminal charges and concluding with a full-blown trial in an Article III court. A second group of critics accepts the President's authority to detain individuals who truly are enemy combatants, but questions whether the executive branch has provided—or is even capable of providing—adequate procedural safeguards for determining who qualifies as an enemy combatant.

Objections to the President's authority to detain enemy combatants, including U.S. citizens and individuals captured on U.S. soil, are without merit. The President's detention authority has a long historical pedigree, and the U.S. Supreme Court has twice affirmed presidential power to detain even U.S. citizens who are enemy combatants. In this essay, we will demonstrate not only that the detention of captured enemy combatants by the military is supported by domestic law and the international law of war, but also that the use of this detention authority makes clear policy sense in the context of the War on Terror. The question of what procedural safeguards the Constitution requires be used in identifying and designating enemy combatants is a more complex question that is still being worked out by the lower courts in the wake of the Supreme Court's decision in *Hamdi v. Rumsfeld*, 542 U.S. ___. We will argue here that the procedural protections the government has put in place since *Hamdi* was decided are sufficient to protect the constitutional liberty interests of both citizen and noncitizen combatants, whether they are held on U.S. soil or abroad.

I. Presidential Power to Detain

The President's power to detain captured enemy combatants derives from his constitutional position as Commander in Chief of the armed forces, and thus depends on the existence of a state of war. There can be little question that the conflict between the United

States and Al Qaeda qualifies as war under both domestic and international law. On November 13, 2001, the President proclaimed that "a state of armed conflict" exists between the United States and Al Qaeda "that requires the use of the United States Armed Forces," a finding that had already been implicitly adopted by Congress shortly after the September 11 attacks when it passed the Authorization for Use of Military Force. 115 Stat. 224. Whether a state of war exists is a question reserved to the political branches, and the courts have historically treated presidential findings on the subject as determinative. *See, e.g., The Prize Cases*, 67 U.S. 635, 670 (1863).

Some critics argue that the conflict between the United States and Al Qaeda cannot constitute "war" under international law because one of the parties to the conflict, Al Qaeda, is not a nation state. This position cannot be squared with historical practice or the text of the major multilateral treaties governing armed conflict. Common Article 3 of the Geneva Conventions, for example, expressly recognizes the existence of "armed conflict[s] not of an international character" to which many of the laws of war concerning the detention of captured enemy combatants apply. The primary factor under international law differentiating between true "armed conflicts" and lesser internal disturbances such as crimes and riots is the level of intensity of the violence. *See* John C. Yoo and James C. Ho, *The Status of Terrorists*, 44 Va. J. Int'l L. 207, 211 (2003). The attacks launched against New York City and Washington, D.C. on September 11 were devastatingly violent, causing approximately 3,000 deaths in a carefully coordinated attempt to cripple the U.S. economy and eliminate key U.S. leadership. They were not an isolated incident, but rather were the most recent phase in a sustained campaign of violence that Al Qaeda has waged against the United States for more than a decade. The political purpose of the attacks, the massive damage they inflicted, and the United States' swift military response renders the conflict with Al Qaeda an "armed conflict" under the international law of war, and NATO, Australia, and the OAS signaled their agreement shortly after September 11 when they activated mutual self-defense clauses in their treaties with the United States.

Since the conflict between the United States and Al Qaeda qualifies as war under both domestic and international law, the President has constitutional authority as Commander in Chief to order that enemy combatants captured during the course of the conflict be detained. Wald and Onek do not seriously dispute this contention, but rather attempt to carve out an exception from the President's general detention authority with this somewhat mystifying argument: "The extension of this customary law to the situation of a U.S. citizen detained in this country who was not an enemy soldier or had not been captured on the battlefield has never been sanctioned by our courts or by international law or practice."

If Wald and Onek mean only what they have literally stated—that U.S. citizens who are not associated with Al Qaeda cannot legally be detained by the executive as enemy combatants—then their argument is a non sequitur, as the Bush Administration has never purported to possess, much less exercise, such an authority. If, on the other hand, Wald and Onek mean to suggest that the military detentions of Yaser Esam Hamdi and Jose Padilla are of a sort that has never been sanctioned by U.S. courts or by international law, then they are simply wrong.

In *Ex Parte Quirin*, 317 U.S. 1 (1942), the Supreme Court upheld the detention and trial by military commission of eight Nazi agents who were captured on U.S. soil, all of whom had previously resided in the United States and one of whom was a U.S. citizen. In *Hamdi*, the Court affirmed presidential power to detain a U.S. citizen captured on the battlefield in Afghanistan and held within the United States. The Court explained that "universal agreement and practice" support the President's authority to capture and detain individuals who are "part of or supporting forces hostile to the United States . . . and engaged in an armed conflict against the United States," and found that "[a] citizen, no less than an alien," can fall into this category. 542 U.S. at ___. Because citizens pose the same threat as aliens "of returning to the front during the ongoing conflict," there is "no bar to this Nation's holding one of its own citizens as an enemy combatant," and like aliens, they may be held "for the duration of the relevant conflict." *Id.* at ___.

Since the President's authority to detain a citizen in Hamdi's circumstances has already been upheld by the Supreme Court, one can surmise that Wald and Onek must be objecting to the detention of Jose Padilla. According to the Department of Justice, Padilla trained at the Al Farouq terrorist training camp in Afghanistan; received additional training in explosives on a subsequent trip to Afghanistan; presented a plan to senior Al Qaeda leadership to detonate a dirty bomb in the United States; and was ultimately sent into the United States by senior Al Qaeda leader Khalid Sheik Mohammad, supplied with cash and travel documents, for the purpose of blowing up apartment buildings and exploring the viability of his scheme to detonate a dirty bomb. Padilla is virtually indistinguishable from the U.S. citizen whose detention was upheld in Quirin, as both "associate[d] themselves with the military arm of the enemy government, and with its aid, guidance and direction enter[ed] this country bent on hostile acts." 317 U.S. at 37-38. Assuming that Padilla cannot rebut these charges in accordance with the procedures discussed below, the government's authority to detain him as an enemy combatant is beyond question.

Despite the existence of this authority, Wald and Onek question whether "our experience" with post-9/11 terrorism suggests that it is actually wise to detain individuals as enemy combatants rather than resorting to traditional law enforcement authorities. Their experience of post-9/11 terrorism, of course, is one of having been kept safe from further terrorist attacks for a period of more than three years by the authorities the government has chosen to exercise, a far different experience from that of law enforcement officers who have struggled to bring traditional criminal authorities to bear on circumstances they were not really designed to address.

One need not resort to hypotheticals to demonstrate the propriety of invoking a war powers paradigm in the present conflict, however: merely look at the case of Yaser Esam Hamdi. A U.S. citizen by virtue of having been born in Louisiana, Hamdi left the United States as a small child when his parents moved to Saudi Arabia and lived the rest of his life abroad. At some point he moved to Afghanistan and became associated with the Taliban, with whom he was fighting when he was captured on the field of battle sometime in 2001. The United States had a great interest in detaining Hamdi until the end of the conflict in Afghanistan to prevent him from rejoining enemy forces. The United States does not, however, regard Hamdi as a criminal; he had limited ties to the United States and was essentially unaware of his status as a U.S. citizen. Yet Wald and Onek would require that Hamdi either be tried for treason, which carries a minimum penalty of five years' imprisonment, or released on his own cognizance, neither of which option is particularly palatable. Traditional criminal authorities may at times provide important weapons to be used against terrorists and their use certainly should not be ruled out, but they are too often ill-suited to a conflict that is best described as a war, and thus ought not supply the governing paradigm.

II. Procedural Safeguards

In *Hamdi*, the Supreme Court ruled that a U.S. citizen who is detained as an enemy combatant for a prolonged period of time must be afforded "notice of the factual basis for his classification" and "a fair opportunity to rebut the Government's factual assertions before a neutral decisionmaker." 542 U.S. ___. The Court further ruled that citizens "unquestionably ha[ve] the right to access to counsel in connection with [such] proceedings."

Although *Hamdi* was billed by many as a substantial defeat for the government, the Court in fact showed substantial recognition for the need to defer to the Executive in times of war. Specifically, the Court adopted an unusual "presumption in favor of the Government's evidence," and further held that the Government should be permitted to rely on hearsay evidence when the production of a witness would be burdensome to the war effort. *Id.* at ___. Significantly, the Court also broadly hinted that the requisite neutral decision maker could be "an appropriately authorized and properly constituted military tribunal," which would allow the Executive to keep enemy combatant determinations entirely within the executive branch.

This novel procedural arrangement finds little support in constitutional text or history, but it does strike a delicate balance between the need to protect citizens from the threat of executive tyranny, on the one hand, and the need to permit the President to vigorously prosecute the war effort on the other. Unfortunately, the procedures have yet to be tested in practice, as Hamdi was released to Saudi Arabia on the condition that he not leave the country, and Padilla has chosen to contest the President's authority to detain him rather than the factual basis for his detention. At this point, it seems likely that the government will ultimately elect to provide detained U.S. citizens with military hearings similar to those being employed with respect to the noncitizen detainees being held at Guantanamo, with the most significant exception being a more robust role for the participation of counsel.

III. Immigration Violations and Material Witness Warrants

Wald and Onek strongly object to the government's use of immigration detention authorities and material witness warrants to detain suspected terrorists in the immediate aftermath of the September 11 attacks. Specifically, they complain that many immigrants were detained because of "technical" immigration violations, and that some individuals were detained as material witnesses even though the government acknowledged that it "may" turn out that they had no useful information.

These are not, by and large, complaints of illegality. The DOJ Inspector General found that all but one of the 762 aliens taken into custody by the Department violated immigration laws, and the material witness statute does not, as Wald and Onek imply, require that the government be certain that an individual knows material information before they may be detained for the purpose of securing their testimony. Wald and Onek's complaint invokes a deeper policy question whether it is appropriate to use all available legal authorities to fight terrorism, including ones that were not expressly designed for that purpose.

Although we would not defend every instance of the Department's activities, such as the physical abuse of some detainees by rogue prison guards, we would suggest that the Department's overarching strategy to employ all available legal authorities to disrupt potential terrorist plots was entirely responsible. In laying out the strategy, Attorney General John Ashcroft invoked Robert Kennedy's famous campaign against organized crime, when it was said that mobsters would be arrested, if necessary, for "spitting on the sidewalk." What's good for the mob ought to be good for terrorists. Indeed, the need for such a strategy has perhaps never been so great as it was in the weeks immediately following September 11, when it was clear that our intelligence sources had failed us and the immediate priority had to be to remove suspected terrorists from the streets.

Patricia Wald and Joe Onek

_____

Response

Words matter. The only kinds of "enemy combatant" for whom the Supreme Court has upheld detention outside the normal criminal processes are prisoners of war and those, like Hamdi, who were (allegedly) captured on or near the battlefield while engaged in armed conflict against the United States or its allies, and then only after the opportunity in a due process hearing to rebut the definitional status. (Justices Scalia and Stevens went further and said that a full-blown treason trial would be necessary for a U.S. citizen captured on the battlefield.) The *Quirin* case involved German soldiers, including a U.S. citizen, who were given a trial before a military commission. Neither case remotely resembles the situation of Padilla, whose provocative history as recounted by Jacob and Yoo is based entirely on the government's untied charges. Moreover, according to Administration lawyers in open court, the government's unilateral power to detain people in military custody would extend far beyond Padilla to a person who simply donates money to a terrorist organization. Nothing in the Court's decisions supports such an expansive definition of "enemy combatant." It is also mistaken to say, as Jacob and Yoo do, that the Court in *Hamdi* "adopted" as adequate procedures for a citizen detainee a presumption in favor of the government's evidence or a military hearing; those options were suggestive only and not concurred in by a majority of justices. Indeed, two justices who went with the plurality to permit a hearing for Hamdi on remand specifically rejected them.

For the moment and at least until Congress legislates on the subject, the definition of a detainable enemy combatant should remain where the Court left it—an enemy soldier (as in *Quirin*) or a person captured on the battlefield and engaged in armed conflict against the United States (as in *Hamdi*). That is the only definition recognized by the Geneva Convention and in international law. Any legislative extension should be subjected to robust debate and to a demonstration of need, a demonstration Jacob and Yoo do not bother to make.

Jacob and Yoo are also too cavalier about the roundup and detention of immigrants in the immediate wake of 9/11. They cite Robert Kennedy's statement that he planned to arrest mobsters for spitting on the sidewalk. But, as John Zogby has pointed out, the Administration did not arrest terrorists for spitting; it arrested spitters—i.e., persons with (often minor) immigration violations—and treated them like terrorists. While some overreach may have been inevitable in the first days after the terrorist attacks, the failure of the Administration and its supporters to fully acknowledge the abuses committed is a troubling portent for any future mass detention situation.

John Yoo and Gregory Jacob

The Last Word

Words do indeed matter. They also speak for themselves. Wald and Onek assert that "the definition of a detainable enemy combatant" is limited under both international law and Supreme Court precedent to "an enemy soldier . . . or a person captured on the battlefield and engaged in armed conflict against the United States." Yet the Geneva Convention on Prisoners of War expressly states that "supply contractors" and "war correspondents" accompanying armed forces may be treated as prisoners of war, as may "crews . . . of the merchant marine and . . . civil aircraft of the Parties to the conflict"—whether they accompany armed forces or not. GPW Article 4(4)-(5). Similarly, in *Hamdi* the Supreme Court held that the President may detain any individual who is "part of *or supporting* forces . . . engaged in armed conflict against the United States." 542 U.S. at ___ (emphasis added).

As to the detention of potential terror suspects for immigration violations in the wake of 9/11, we reiterate our condemnation of any abuses but reaffirm our assessment that the overarching strategy was on balance appropriate. The Justice Department did not indiscriminately detain all immigration law violators, as Wald and Onek imply, but rather focused its efforts on individuals tied to terror suspects and held them only as long as was necessary to determine they were not a threat.

Material Support

David Cole
Paul Rosenzweig

Summary

Mary DeRosa

18 U.S.C. 2339B prohibits "providing material support or re-sources" to an organization the Secretary of State has designated as a "foreign terrorist organization." The material support ban was first passed as part of the Antiterrorism and Effective Death Penalty Act of 1996 (AEDPA). The provision's purpose is to deny terrorist groups the ingredients necessary for planning and carrying out attacks. Congress was concerned that terrorist organizations with charitable or humanitarian arms were raising funds within the United States that could then be used to further their terrorist activities. The provision outlawed any support to these groups, irrespective of whether that support was intended for humanitarian purposes.

The original definition of "material support or resources" in the AEDPA included providing tangible support such as money, goods, and materials and also less concrete support, such as "personnel" and "training." Section 805 of the PATRIOT Act expanded the definition to include "expert advice or assistance." Some courts have found the terms "personnel," "training," and "expert advice or assistance" to be unconstitutionally vague. The courts have reasoned that enforcement of these provisions has the potential to criminalize First Amendment–protected speech.

The Intelligence Reform and Terrorism Prevention Act of 2004, signed into law in December 2004, responded to these courts by providing more detailed definitions of the terms "personnel," "training," and "expert advice or assistance" (section 6603(b)). The Intelligence Reform Act also amended the material support provision to require that to be found to have provided "material support or resources" to a designated terrorist organization, a person must have "knowledge that the organization is a designated terrorist organization . . . that the organization has engaged or engages in terrorist activity . . . or that the organization has engaged or engages in terrorism" (section 6603(c)(2)).

David Cole

Criminalizing Speech: The Material Support Provision

Defenders of the USA PATRIOT Act often assert that there have been no abuses under the Act. That all depends on what you consider an abuse. In the name of cutting off "material support" for terrorist organizations, section 805(a)(2) criminalizes pure speech, penalizing the provision of "expert advice" to proscribed organizations, even where the advice has no connection whatsoever to any terrorist activity. It bans speech without requiring any of the showings that the Supreme Court has deemed essential before speech may be constitutionally punished. It should not be surprising that this was the first provision of the PATRIOT Act to be declared unconstitutional. *Humanitarian Law Project v. Ashcroft* (HLP), 309 F. Supp. 2d 1185, 1200 (C.D. Cal. 2004).

Moreover, the abuses are not hypothetical. This provision has already served as the basis for the prosecution of a college student for running a Web site that happened to have links to other Web sites, which in turn featured speeches by Muslim sheikhs advocating violent jihad. The prosecution's theory was that the student was providing material support in the form of "expert advice or assistance" by running the Web site and linking it to such statements. On the government's view, it did not need to prove that the student intended to further violence of any kind by including these links on

144

his Web site. On that understanding of the law, *The New York Times* could be prosecuted for featuring a link to Osama bin Laden's latest taped statement in connection with a story about the statement. An Idaho jury, apparently more attuned to First Amendment values than the U.S. government, acquitted the student.

Ironically, when Congress adopted this provision, it labored under the impression that it was drafted much more narrowly than the government now treats it. The House Committee on the Judiciary reported that "[T]he definition of providing material support to terrorists in title 18 is expanded to include providing 'expert advice or assistance.' *This will only be a crime if it is provided 'knowing or intending that [the expert advice or assistance] be used in preparation for, or in carrying out,' any 'Federal terrorism offense.'*" H.R. Rep. No. 107-236(I) at 71 (2001) (emphasis added). Similarly, the Section-by-Section Analysis of the USA PATRIOT Act presented to the Senate stated that the amendment to the definition of material support would "*prohibit[ ] providing terrorists with 'expert advice or assistance,' such as flight training, knowing or intending that it will be used to prepare for or carry out an act of terrorism.*" 147 Cong. Rec. S10990-02, *S11013 (2001) (emphasis added). Yet the government has taken the position that the statute criminalizes the provision of all "expert advice or assistance," even if the advice or assistance has no connection whatsoever to any act of terrorism. Thus, putting aside its serious constitutional defects, this provision should be amended to reflect the intentions of the Congress that initially adopted it.

The PATRIOT Act's prohibition on providing "expert advice or assistance" to proscribed groups amends a preexisting law, enacted as part of the 1996 Anti-Terrorism and Effective Death Penalty Act, which broadly proscribed the provision of "material support" to designated "terrorist organizations." The PATRIOT Act provision's infirmities build on the problems with the 1996 law. That law imposes guilt by association, because it holds people liable not for engaging in, conspiring to engage in, or even aiding or abetting terrorist activity, but instead for supporting even wholly lawful and nonviolent activities of a proscribed group. Had this law been in effect in the 1980s, the tens of thousands of Americans who supported the African National Congress's largely nonviolent anti-apartheid work could have faced criminal prosecution, because the State Department designated the African National Congress a "terrorist" organization until it came to power in South Africa. The PATRIOT Act exacerbates the constitutional infirmities in the material support statute, because it explicitly singles out pure speech—"expert advice"—for criminal prohibition.

The PATRIOT Act provision violates four constitutional principles. First, it contravenes the First Amendment by criminalizing speech without satisfying the constitutional requirements set forth in *Brandenburg v. Ohio*, 395 U.S. 444, 447-48 (1969). In *Brandenburg*, the Supreme Court held that the government may penalize speech only if it is "directed to inciting or producing imminent lawless action and is likely to incite or produce such action." 395 U.S. at 447-48. The USA PATRIOT Act prohibition contains no Brandenburg limitation, but penalizes all "expert advice and assistance," without regard to whether it has anything to do with lawless activity, much less whether it is intended and likely to produce imminent illegal conduct.

Second, the provision violates the First Amendment's right of association, for it criminalizes the provision of advice only when offered to certain disfavored political organizations. Thus, it is perfectly lawful to provide unlimited "expert advice and assistance" to the Palestine Liberation Organization and the Irish Republican Army, because those groups have not been "designated." But if the same advice is offered to the Kurdistan Workers' Party, the speech is criminalized. What triggers the penalty is not the advice itself, but to whom it is offered. This is guilt by association.

In a series of cases involving the Communist Party and other groups, the Supreme Court has consistently held that the only way to avoid guilt by association when punishing someone for his connection to a group is to require proof that the individual "specifically intended" to further the unlawful ends of the group. *See, e.g., Scales,*

146

367 U.S. 203 (1961). Yet the government maintains that the "expert advice" prohibition requires no such showing of intent to further illegal activities. On this view, a human rights activist who seeks to offer a group expert advice in human rights advocacy—in order to persuade the group to use peaceful rather than violent means to further its ends—would face a 15-year prison sentence, and would have no defense even if he could prove that his support in fact reduced the group's reliance on violence. *See* HLP, 309 F. Supp. 2d 1185.

Third, the "expert advice or assistance" ban violates the Fifth Amendment's requirement that criminal penalties must be based on "personal guilt." As the Supreme Court has explained:

> In our jurisprudence guilt is personal, and when the imposition of punishment on . . . conduct can only be justified by reference to the relationship of that . . . conduct to other concededly criminal activity . . . that relationship must be sufficiently substantial to satisfy the concept of personal guilt.

Scales, 367 U.S. at 224. In order to satisfy the "personal guilt" requirement, the Court reasoned, the government must show that the defendant intended to further the group's illegal activities, the same showing required to satisfy the First Amendment. In keeping with this view, even the most expansive federal criminal laws that impose liability based on one's support of another's illegal activity—including RICO, conspiracy laws, and aiding and abetting statutes—all require some proof of intent to further some illegal activity. Yet the government maintains that the material support statute contains no such requirement.

Finally, the ban on providing "expert advice or assistance" is unconstitutionally vague. As one court has already held, the term fails to provide the ordinary person with any real guidance as to which advice is permissible and which is proscribed. HLP, 309 F. Supp. 2d 1185. In the Intelligence Reform and Terrorism Prevention Act of 2004, Congress sought to address this concern by defining "expert advice or assistance" as that advice or assistance which is based on "specialized knowledge." But that definition does no more than offer a slightly more wordy synonym for "expert." It provides no additional clarity, and in fact exacerbates the statute's vagueness, because now an individual must guess as to whether the knowledge that makes his advice "expert" is "specialized" or not.

The statute's defenders often respond that all support for "terrorist organizations," even that targeted exclusively at lawful, nonviolent activities, may free up the organization's resources for terrorist ends. On this view, the provision of expert advice on nonviolent resistance may be criminalized, because it allows the organization to spend resources it would otherwise have spent learning about nonviolence on guns, bullets, or bombs. That argument plainly proves too much. Congress itself does not believe it, for it expressly permits individuals to donate unlimited amounts of medicine and religious materials to designated groups. Moreover, if that view were accepted, it would be unconstitutional for the state to offer any assistance whatsoever to private religious schools, because even assistance strictly limited to secular purposes may free up resources that can then be used for religious ends.

Defenders similarly argue that the provision of "material support" is different from membership per se, and therefore hinging a criminal penalty on material support does not amount to guilt by association. But if that were true, all of the McCarthy-era laws found invalid for imposing guilt by association could have simply been rewritten to penalize not membership, but the payment of dues, or the volunteering of one's time. If the right of association means only the right to join a group that one has no right to support in any material way, including through one's speech, the right would be an empty formality.

Cutting off funding for terrorist activity is unquestionably a legitimate end. But it must be pursued through legitimate means. We have effectively targeted and prosecuted international drug cartels and organized crime organizations without dispensing with the principle of personal guilt and relying on guilt by association. We can and should be able to use similar tools to target those who support terrorism. And we should not be treating as a terrorist a human rights activist who seeks only to provide advice on nonviolent resistance. Yet that is what section 805(a)(2), as interpreted by the government, does.

Paul Rosenzweig

Teaching a Terrorist How to Build a Bomb Is Not Free Speech

The material support provisions of the PATRIOT Act (section 805) are not new. They are derived from pre-9/11 law and are designed, at the core, to prevent individuals from providing money, weapons, and military training to organizations, like Al Quaeda, that intend harm to American citizens.

Poorly executed, section 805 might trench on the fundamental right to openly criticize the government. It could be implemented in a manner that would impinge on First Amendment freedoms in its effort to achieve the legitimate end of cutting off funding and material support for terrorist organizations. But fear of that possibility is a far cry from reality.

And the reality is that such concerns are more theoretical than actual. To be sure, some organizations contend that there are humanitarian aspects to their work and that their humanitarian efforts are distinct from the allegedly terrorist acts of related organizations. They thus argue that the prohibition on material support impinges on First Amendment freedoms of speech and association for their supporters, allowing them to be criminally prosecuted when all they are doing is providing material support to the humanitarian aspects of the organization.

The law, however, understands and respects this concern. Congress recognized the problem when it first passed the material support provisions. It's made clear that "[t]he First Amendment protects one's right to associate with groups that are involved in both legal and illegal activities." That report emphasized that the contemplated ban on material support "does not attempt to restrict a

149

person's right to join an organization. Rather, the restriction only affects one's contribution of financial or material resources to a foreign organization that has been designated as a threat to the national security of the United States." In short, Congress has carefully constructed a balanced and nuanced approach that both recognizes the liberty interests at stake and understands the necessity of enhanced prosecutorial authority.

And the need for greater prosecutorial authority is palpable. For money is fungible. And terrorist organizations do not respect the legal niceties of distinct corporate structures. As a consequence, contributions to the humanitarian aspects of an organization are readily "passed through" to the terrorist arms of related organizations. If this indirect support for terrorism were all that we sought to prevent, the material support laws would be justified.

But the reality is far more insidious—for "humanitarian" assistance by terrorist organizations is often just a code word for efforts to propagate terrorist ideology. Through seemingly beneficial activities like schooling, terrorist organizations teach their vision and win the loyalty of those whom they would control. Truly humanitarian organizations would, one would think, disassociate themselves from the terrorist reality, rather than support it—but alas they do not.

Thus, the idea that there are "wholly lawful and nonviolent activities of proscribed groups" is, I submit, a non sequitur. Proscribed groups, by their nature, have no "wholly lawful" activities—only interests principally intended to further their unlawful ends. Even in distributing tsunami aid in Sri Lanka following the recent disaster there, the Tamil Tigers, who have engaged in a brutal, vicious, and violent rebellion for more than a dozen years, linked their humanitarian relief efforts to their unlawful terror campaign against the Sri Lankan government. To separate the humanitarian from the terrorist is an artificial distinction only a lawyer could accept.

Despite the agreed-upon necessity of defunding truly terrorist organizations, my colleague in this debate believes that the law goes too far in attempting to achieve this end. The arguments against section 805 take three basic forms—that it is discriminatory; that it is vague; and that it is overbroad. The opening essay in this series makes all three arguments—but in the end, they are not persuasive.

Consider, first, discrimination. To be sure, terrorism is a term without rigid definition. And the opening essay in this exchange makes much of the disparate treatment given different terrorist organizations—contrasting the treatment of the Kurdistan Workers' Party with the Irish Republican Army today. But the disparity derives not from a desire to suppress disfavored political views—it derives directly from the objective reality of current affairs. No less an authoritative group than the 9/11 Commission has identified the threat to America as that of "radical Islamists" and their allies. Our policies should recognize that reality—and only a hyperskeptic of government would see in drawing that distinction a purely political motivation. Indeed, as long as those organizations designated have a right to contest their designation in court (as they do), there will exist constraints on the government's ability to arbitrarily act for political reasons.

My colleague also challenges the law as vague. And we can agree that criminal prohibitions must give a person of ordinary intelligence "fair warning" of criminality. But the law does not need to define an offense with mathematical certainty, it need only provide "relatively clear guidelines as to prohibited conduct." *Posters N' Things, Ltd. v. United States*, 511 U.S. 513, 525 (1994). This doctrine recognizes that some exercise of prosecutorial discretion in choosing cases is inevitable—all that the Constitution requires is that Congress, through the text of the statutes, "establish[es] minimal guidelines to govern law enforcement." *Kolender v. Lawson*, 461 U.S. 352, 358 (1983).

The terms chosen by Congress—"personnel," "training," and "expert advice"—are sufficiently clear in their meaning (especially after their amplification in the recent Intelligence reform bill) to provide fair warning to a person of reasonable intelligence as to the potential that his or her conduct falls within the statutory prohibition. The term "personnel," for example, generally describes employees or others affiliated with a particular organization and working under that organization's direction or control. It is used in numerous other places in the criminal code. *E.g.,* 18 U.S.C. § 7(9)(B) ("United States personnel" assigned to a foreign mission or entities); 18 U.S.C. § 31(5)(A) ("ground personnel" preparing an aircraft for flight); 18 U.S.C. § 207(c) ("senior personnel" of executive branch and independent agencies).

Similarly, the ban against providing "training" to designated foreign terrorist organizations is not unconstitutionally vague. The verb "train" is commonly understood to mean: "To subject to discipline and instruction for the purpose of forming the character and developing the powers of, or of making proficient in some occupation." It boggles the mind to suggest that Congress cannot proscribe teaching foreign terrorists how to become better terrorists— yet if the logic of the vagueness argument is followed, that would be the result. And the same is true of allegedly vague phrase "expert assistance." It is a common concept in the law—for example, Rule 702 of the Federal Rules of Evidence defines "expert" testimony to be based on "scientific, technical, or other specialized knowledge." The Oxford English Dictionary offers a similar definition: "One whose special knowledge or skill causes him to be regarded as an authority; a specialist." To deny that those words have meaning is to adopt a Sartrean view of meaning that the law generally rejects.

The real fear of critics, it seems, is the problem of overbreadth— that is, the fear that the existence of this law will chill legitimate free expression. Again, the fear is theoretically plausible. But even the possibility of individual injustice is not a basis for invalidating the law in all its applications. As the Supreme Court recently said, "There comes a point at which the chilling effect of an overbroad law, significant though it may be, cannot justify prohibiting all enforcement of that law—particularly a law that reflects 'legitimate state interests in maintaining comprehensive controls over harmful, constitutionally unprotected conduct.'" *Virginia v. Hicks*, 123 S. Ct. 2191, 2197 (2003).

And this, at the core, demonstrates why the challenge to section 805 should fail. There are no reports of systematic abuse—no public advocates criminalized for their political speech. And the social costs of declaring these laws unconstitutional is potentially catastrophic. The United States has a "legitimate state interest" in controlling the "constitutionally unprotected conduct" of providing material support for terrorism—teaching a terrorist how to build a bomb is not protected free speech.

We cannot afford to stint in our efforts against terrorism based upon unrealized fears. More than a half dozen criminal cases have been brought under the material support provisions of the law. They include cases like that of Mohammed Junneh Barbar, who was arrested in America while trying to set up a training and recruitment camp to institute a bombing campaign. Others involve defendants who have taken jihad training in Afghanistan, or facilitated communications between jailed terrorists and their supporters overseas.

The material support provisions deal with a new reality—a reality where we cannot afford to wait for the terrorist crime to occur before acting and a reality where the nature of support for terrorists is variable and changing. To accept my colleague's reasoning and deem the statute unconstitutional is to despair of any real ability to address this conduct—and that is, regretfully, a result we simply cannot afford.

If, as George Santayana said, "Those who forget history are doomed to repeat it," then it is equally true that "those who are obsessed with history are doomed never to escape it." Those opposed to the terrorist material support provisions of the PATRIOT Act seem, at times, obsessed with history. Witness the companion essay's dated references to McCarthyism. But we live in a different time now—one where an activist press, public interest groups, Congress, and the courts all make systematic political abuse substantially less likely. The fears are plausible—but they are not reality. More important, they are (or ought to be) of no legal moment, since the mere potential for application of an overly broad law is not enough to invalidate it.

David Cole

Tilting at Straw Men

The title of Paul Rosenzweig's defense of the material support statute is telling: "Teaching a Terrorist How to Build a Bomb Is Not Free Speech." Has anyone argued that teaching terrorists to build bombs is protected speech? No. As my critique made clear, supporting a terrorist organization with intent to further its illegal activities is not protected by the First Amendment, and can and should be criminalized. If the material support statute stopped there, it would pose no constitutional difficulties.

Similarly, if the statute made it a crime to give money to a terrorist organization's lawful activities with knowledge or intent that the money will be "passed through" to the group's terrorist arm, as Rosenzweig puts it, or with knowledge or intent that the organization's "humanitarian activities" are used to advance terrorist activity, it would pose no constitutional difficulty. That is essentially the theory behind the anti-racketeering law's criminalization of fronts used to launder or cover up illegal activities, and that law does not trench on First Amendment freedoms.

But the material support statute does not stop there. It criminalizes virtually all support of groups designated terrorist, even if the defendant can prove that his support was not intended to further terrorist activities, did not in fact further any terrorism, and actually reduced terrorist activities by encouraging the use of nonviolent means. The analogy would be a racketeering law that made it a crime to support wholly lawful activities of an entity that also engaged in crime, even where the supporter had no intent to further the enterprise's illegal activities. Such a law, the Supreme Court has repeatedly made clear, would impermissibly impose guilt by association.

Rosenzweig relies, as do all defenders of the statute, on the contention that money is fungible, and therefore support even of the lawful activities of a designated group theoretically frees up resources that can be used for illegal ends. But Congress itself does not take that view, as it expressly allows unlimited donations of very fungible medicine to designated groups, and also allows the Secretary of State to approve the provision of expert advice, training, and personnel to designated terrorist groups. If Rosenzweig's fungibility principle held, the ban should have no exceptions.

In addition, as noted in my opening essay, fungibility proves too much. If accepted, it would never be permissible for a state to provide any support to religious schools, because any support, even of wholly secular functions, frees up money that the school can then spend inculcating religion. Similarly, it would be constitutional to ban all donations to Greenpeace, Operation Rescue, the Socialist Workers Party, or any other entity that has ever engaged in any illegal activities, without any showing that the donor sought to further the group's illegal as opposed to legal ends. Finally, the "fungibility" argument would make the Supreme Court's prohibition on guilt by association a meaningless formality. To say that one has the right to join a group, but that it is a crime to provide the group with any support whatsoever, whether through dues, contributions, or even volunteering one's time, is not, as Rosenzweig argues, "a balanced and nuanced approach that recognizes the liberty interests at stake," but a blatant ruse that takes away with one hand what it says it is preserving with the other.

Paul Rosenzweig

Some Straw Men Are Really Made of Steel

My colleague David Cole says I am destroying a straw man. Of course, he agrees, teaching a terrorist to build a bomb is not protected free speech. And, of course, he argues, giving money with the intent to support terrorist activities can be proscribed. These are, he argues, not the problem—rather, in Cole's view, the problem is that the fungibility argument proves too much (since Congress itself did not prohibit all fungible assistance to terrorist organizations) and with the potential prosecution of those who can prove that their money was not used for terrorist acts. Neither argument persuades.

With regard to the fungibility argument, this is, with respect, just another form of the common (and unpersuasive) argument that a legislature is not competent to make distinctions within classes of conduct. Congress may differentiate between medicines and money, judging the potential for abuse of the latter lower and the humanitarian benefits greater. Cole simply repudiates that judgment. But international law has long recognized this distinction. As long ago as the 1907 London Convention on blockades, the international community recognized the difference between absolute contraband, conditional contraband (whose prohibition was evaluated in context), and non-contraband (that could never be blockaded). Congress, by extending the concept of contraband to money, has merely recognized in the terrorism context that which we have long understood in the criminal context of our money-laundering laws—money is the lifeblood of illegal enterprises.

More fundamentally, this argument is a red herring. For if Cole thinks that the distinction between medicine and money is untenable, it would be a sufficient answer for Congress to prohibit all support to banned organizations, including medicines. Yet one strongly suspects that Cole would reject that response.

Rather, the main dispute lies in Cole's argument that the law permits potential prosecutions where the money provided was not used for terrorist acts. The argument has several flaws.

Most saliently, the likely scope of this objection is the null set. Given the fungibility of money, unless one can prove that the recipient organization engages in no terrorist acts whatsoever (a situation that is not of concern to either Cole or myself, inasmuch as those organizations are not on the prohibited list), then it is impossible to prove that none of the money was converted to illegal use.

More important, this argument is not one for the blanket invalidation of a law that has proved useful in any number of perfectly reasonable prosecutions. The fear of mistaken prosecution is a theoretically legitimate one—but given the infrequency with which individual injustice is likely to occur, we must recognize, as the Supreme Court has, that potential overbreadth typically does not prohibit all enforcement of a law.

Finally, Cole's argument about protected expenditures of money on behalf of "good speech" simply proves too much. If his argument were correct, then it would be unlawful for the United States to embargo a country entirely, as we did with South Africa. Surely, one would argue, conflict resolution training money should be allowed to the apartheid régime. Yet nobody made that argument in the 1980s and to repeat it today is to realize how hollow it sounds. There are some organizations and nations that are beyond the pale—and the material support laws appropriately recognize that fact.

Contributors

Stewart Baker is the current chair of the ABA's Standing Committee on Law and National Security, and is a partner with Steptoe & Johnson LLP. He is currently serving as the general counsel of the Commission on the Intelligence Capabilities of the United States Regarding Weapons of Mass Destruction. He also serves on the President's Export Council Subcommittee on Export Administration. Previously, Mr. Baker served as general counsel of the National Security Agency, member and acting chair of the President's Export Council Subcommittee on Encryption, deputy general counsel of the Education Department, and law clerk to Justice Stevens of the U.S. Supreme Court.

David Cole is a professor of law at the Georgetown University Law Center. After graduating from law school, Professor Cole served as a law clerk to Judge Arlin M. Adams of the U.S. Court of Appeals for the Third Circuit. Professor Cole then became a staff attorney for the Center for Constitutional Rights, where he litigated a number of major First Amendment cases. He continues to litigate First Amendment and other constitutional issues as a volunteer staff attorney at the center. Professor Cole has published in a variety of areas, including civil rights, criminal justice, constitutional law, and law and literature. He wrote on section 218 and Material Support.

James B. Comey currently serves as deputy attorney general for the U.S. Department of Justice. Before assuming that post, Mr. Comey served as United States Attorney for the Southern District of New York from January 2002 to the time of his confirmation. Previously, Mr. Comey served as managing assistant U.S. attorney in charge of the Richmond Division of the United States Attorney's Office for the Eastern District of Virginia. As U.S. attorney, Mr. Comey oversaw numerous terrorism cases and supervised prosecutions of executives of WorldCom, Adelphia, and Imclone on fraud and securities-related charges. Mr. Comey also created a specialized unit devoted to prosecuting international drug cartels. As an assistant U.S. attorney in the Eastern District of Virginia, he handled the Khobar Towers terrorist bombing case, arising from the June 1996 attack on a U.S. military facility in Saudi Arabia in which 19 airmen were killed. Mr. Comey wrote an introduction to this project.

James X. Dempsey is the executive director of the Center for Democracy & Technology. He works on privacy and electronic surveillance issues and heads CDT's international project, the Global Internet Policy Initiative. Before joining CDT, Mr. Dempsey was deputy director for the Center for National Security Studies. Mr. Dempsey previously worked on Capitol Hill as assistant counsel to the House Judiciary Subcommittee on Civil and Constitutional Rights, where his primary areas of responsibility included oversight of the FBI, privacy, and civil liberties. Mr. Dempsey wrote on sections 206, 209, 212, 213, and 220.

Mary DeRosa is a senior fellow in the Technology and Public Policy Program at the Center for Strategic and International Studies. Previously, she served on the National Security Council staff (1997-2001) as special assistant to the president and legal adviser and, earlier, as deputy legal adviser. From 1995 to 1997, she was special counsel to the general counsel at the Department of Defense, and in 1994 she was an attorney for the Advisory Board on the Investigative Capability of the Department of Defense. Before joining the government, Ms. DeRosa was a lawyer in private practice at the Washington, D.C., and Los Angeles offices of Arnold & Porter. She was a law clerk to the Honorable Richard J. Cardamone on the U.S. Court of Appeals for the Second Circuit and is a graduate of George Washington University's Law School and the University of Virginia. She has written short descriptions of each provision.

Contributors

Viet Dinh is a professor of law at the Georgetown University Law Center. Professor Dinh served as assistant attorney general for Legal Policy at the U.S. Department of Justice from 2001 to 2003. As the official responsible for federal legal policy, he conducted a comprehensive review of DOJ priorities, policies, and practices after 9/11, and played a key role in developing the USA PATRIOT Act. Professor Dinh has also served as Associate Special Counsel to the U.S. Senate Whitewater Committee, as special counsel to Senator Pete V. Domenici for the Impeachment Trial of President Clinton, and as counsel to the special master in *In re* Austrian and German Bank Holocaust Litigation. After graduating from Harvard Law School, where he was a class marshal and an Olin Research Fellow in Law and Economics, Professor Dinh was a law clerk to Judge Laurence H. Silberman of the U.S. Court of Appeals for the D.C. Circuit and U.S. Supreme Court Justice Sandra Day O'Connor.

Timothy H. Edgar is a legislative counsel for the American Civil Liberties Union in its Washington National Office. Mr. Edgar is responsible for defending civil liberties in Congress and in the executive branch in the areas of national security, terrorism, and immigration. Mr. Edgar has testified before Congress and the U.S. Commission on Civil Rights on anti-terrorism legislation and intelligence reform. He has published articles and also addresses these topics in panels and in radio and television appearances. A graduate with honors of both Dartmouth College and Harvard Law School, Mr. Edgar was a law clerk to Judge Sandra L. Lynch of the United States Court of Appeals for the First Circuit. He left private practice to join the ACLU in May 2001. Mr. Edgar wrote on Borders.

Robert J. Grey, Jr., a partner in the Richmond, Virginia, office of Hunton & Williams, is president of the American Bar Association. Mr. Grey is devoting his term to improving justice through better juries via the American Jury Initiative. Additionally, he is working to review, unify, and update ABA programs to increase diversity in the legal profession, to advance the ABA's international rule of law efforts, and to safeguard the profession's independence. Mr. Grey has long been

161

active in the ABA, as chair of the House of Delegates from 1998-2000 and as a member of the Board of Governors. Throughout his ABA career, he has been active in strategic planning and increasing diversity in the profession. Mr. Grey's law practice is focused on administrative matters before state and federal agencies, mediation and dispute resolution, and legislative representation of clients. Mr. Grey wrote a Welcome on behalf of the American Bar Association.

Gregory Jacob, Deputy Solicitor of Labor, served as deputy policy director for legal matters for the Bush-Cheney '04 campaign. Before joining the campaign, he served as an attorney adviser in the Office of Legal Counsel of the U.S. Department of Justice, where he worked on issues involving war powers, national security, and international law. Mr. Jacob wrote on Detainees.

John J. Kavanagh is an associate in the Washington, D.C., office of Steptoe & Johnson LLP, in the firm's litigation practice group. Before joining the firm, Mr. Kavanagh served for three years as an attorney with the U.S. Navy Judge Advocate General's Corps. Mr. Kavanagh previously worked as a Secretary of Defense Honors Legal Intern in the Department of Defense Office of General Counsel—International Affairs and Intelligence. He has also worked as a special assistant to the assistant U.S. trade representative for Japan and China and as an honors intern with the Federal Bureau of Investigation—National Security Division. Mr. Kavanagh holds a master's degree from the Fletcher School of Law and Diplomacy at Tufts University. Mr. Kavanagh acted as editor of the project.

Orin S. Kerr is a professor of law at the George Washington University Law School, where he teaches criminal law, criminal procedure, and computer crime law. Previously, Professor Kerr served as a trial attorney in the Computer Crime and Intellectual Property Section of the Criminal Division at the U.S. Department of Justice, and also as special assistant U.S. Attorney for the Eastern District of Virginia. He clerked for Judge Leonard I. Garth of the U.S. Court of Appeals for the Third Circuit and Justice Anthony M. Kennedy of the U.S. Supreme Court. Orin Kerr wrote on sections 209, 212, and 220.

Heather Mac Donald is a John M. Olin fellow at the Manhattan Institute and a contributing editor to *City Journal*. Ms. Mac Donald has written on a range of topics including homeland security, policing and "racial" profiling, educational policy, and the New York courts. She is the author of *Are Cops Racist?* and *The Burden of Bad Ideas*. A nonpracticing lawyer, Ms. Mac Donald has clerked for the Honorable Stephen Reinhardt, U.S. Court of Appeals for the Ninth Circuit, has been an attorney-adviser in the Office of the General Counsel for the U.S. Environmental Protection Agency, and was a volunteer with the National Resource Defense Fund in New York City. Ms. Mac Donald wrote on section 213.

Kate Martin has been director of the Center for National Security Studies since 1992, where she has litigated and written about national security and civil liberties issues, including government secrecy, intelligence, terrorism, and enemy combatant detentions. Ms. Martin has taught strategic intelligence and public policy at Georgetown University Law School and also served as general counsel to the National Security Archive, a research library located at George Washington University. Ms. Martin wrote on section 203.

Andrew C. McCarthy is an attorney and a senior fellow at the Foundation for the Defense of Democracies in Washington, D.C., an organization that conducts research and education in national security issues. Previously, Mr. McCarthy was a federal prosecutor for the U.S. Attorney's Office for the Southern District of New York, where he participated in many of the most significant cases in our nation's recent history, particularly in the field of national security. Mr. McCarthy led the prosecution against the terror organization of Sheik Omar Abdel Rahman, in which militants were convicted of conducting a war of urban terror on the United States. Mr. McCarthy also led the litigation over crucial confession evidence, which helped secure convictions for the bombings of the American Embassies in Kenya and Tanzania. Mr. McCarthy wrote on sections 214, 215, and 218.

Joe Onek is senior counsel and director of the Liberty and Security Initiative with The Constitution Project in Washington, D.C. Mr. Onek has worked with a number of political and legal organizations. He served as deputy counsel to the President during the Carter Administration and as principal deputy associate attorney general and State Department Rule of Law Coordinator during the Clinton Administration. Mr. Onek also was a law clerk for Justice William J. Brennan of the U.S. Supreme Court and assistant counsel on the Senate Judiciary Committee. Mr. Onek previously served as the director of the Center of Law and Social Policy. Mr. Onek wrote on Detainees.

Paul Rosenzweig is senior legal research fellow in the Center for Legal and Judicial Studies at the Heritage Foundation, where his research interests focus on issues of civil liberties and national security, criminal law, law enforcement, and legal ethics. Mr. Rosenzweig is also an adjunct professor of Law at George Mason University School of Law, and he has served as a trial attorney in the Environmental Crimes Section of the Department of Justice, as Investigative Counsel to the House Committee on Transportation and Infrastructure, and, most recently, as senior litigation counsel in the Office of the Independent Counsel. Mr. Rosenzweig wrote on section 206 and Material Support.

Suzanne E. Spaulding was recently named as managing director of the Harbour Group, LLC. She previously served as minority staff director for the U.S. House of Representatives Permanent Select Committee on Intelligence. She has been a consultant on national security-related issues, including terrorism, homeland security, critical infrastructure protection security, intelligence, law enforcement, and technology for addressing the threat from biological, nuclear, or radiological weapons. Ms. Spaulding was the executive director of two congressionally mandated commissions, the National Commission on Terrorism and the Commission to Assess the Organization of the Federal Government to Combat the Threat of Weapons of Mass Destruction. Ms. Spaulding wrote on Lone Wolf.

Contributors

Peter P. Swire is a professor of law at the Mortiz College of the Law of Ohio State University, and he also works with the Washington, D.C., office of Morrison & Foerster in a consulting capacity. Previously, Mr. Swire served in the Clinton Administration as Chief Counselor for Privacy, U.S. Office of Management and Budget. He was responsible for coordinating administration policy on public- and private-sector uses of personal information, chaired a White House working group on how to update surveillance laws for the Internet age, and served on the White House Electronic Commerce Working group. Mr. Swire wrote on sections 214 and 215.

George J. Terwilliger III is a senior partner in the Washington, D.C., office of White & Case LLP, where he represents international clients in litigation and special projects. Mr. Terwilliger previously served as deputy attorney general of the United States, U.S. attorney in Vermont, and as a federal prosecutor in Washington, D.C. He regularly participates in fora focused on national security issues, drawing on extensive experience in terrorism and national security matters. Mr. Terwilliger wrote on Borders.

Patricia Wald served on the U.S. Court of Appeals for the District of Columbia from 1979-1991, becoming chief judge in 1986. She previously served as the first vice president for the American Law Institution, and also as a judge on the International Criminal Tribunal for the former Yugoslavia. Judge Wald also chaired the Open Society Institute Justice Initiative and is presently a member of the President's Commission on the Intelligence Capabilities of the United States Regarding Weapons of Mass Destruction. Judge Wald has also served as the assistant attorney general for Legislative Affairs at the Department of Justice. Judge Wald wrote on Detainees.

Michael J. Woods is senior executive vice president for legal affairs with MZM, Inc. in Washington, D.C., where he advises clients on national security law and counterintelligence matters. Before joining MZM, Inc., Mr. Woods served as chief of the National Security Law Unit in the FBI's Office of the General Counsel and as the first principal legal adviser to the new National Counterintelligence Executive. Mr. Woods has also served as a prosecutor in the Justice Department's Environmental Crimes Section, and briefly as a special assistant attorney in the U.S. Attorney's Office for D.C. Mr. Woods wrote on Lone Wolf.

John Yoo is a professor of law at the University of California, Berkeley, School of Law, where he has taught since 1993. Previously, he served as a deputy assistant attorney general in the Office of Legal Counsel of the U.S. Department of Justice, where he worked on issues involving foreign affairs, national security, and the separation of powers. Professor Yoo also served as general counsel of the U.S. Senate Judiciary Committee, and he has clerked for Judge Laurence H. Silberman of the U.S. Court of Appeals of the District of Columbia and for Justice Clarence Thomas of the U.S. Supreme Court. Mr. Yoo wrote on Detainees.

Sally Albertazzie is practice group coordinator of the e-commerce practice group at Steptoe & Johnson LLP, and is the administrator of the companion "sourceblog," www.patriotdebates.com. She has been with Steptoe since 1995 and is a graduate of Georgetown University's paralegal program. Ms. Albertazzie edits and publishes Steptoe's *E-Commerce Law Week*, coordinates the group's workflow, and manages the group's paralegals.

Holly McMahon has been the director of the American Bar Association Standing Committee on Law and National Security for more than 10 years. Previously, she served as the director of government programs for the American Bar Association and, before that, served in the Reagan White House as staff assistant for the Office of Private Sector Initiatives.

Appendix

**Amendments Made By Section 201 of USA PATRIOT Act
(amendments in bold text)**

18 U.S.C. § 2516. Authorization for interception of wire, oral, or electronic communications

(1) The Attorney General, Deputy Attorney General, Associate Attorney General, or any Assistant Attorney General, any acting Assistant Attorney General, or any Deputy Assistant Attorney General or acting Deputy Assistant Attorney General in the Criminal Division specially designated by the Attorney General, may authorize an application to a Federal judge of competent jurisdiction for, and such judge may grant in conformity with section 2518 of this chapter an order authorizing or approving the interception of wire or oral communications by the Federal Bureau of Investigation, or a Federal agency having responsibility for the investigation of the offense as to which the application is made, when such interception may provide or has provided evidence of—

. . . .

(q) any criminal violation of section 229 (relating to chemical weapons); or sections 2332, 2332a, 2332b, 2332d, 2332f, 2339A, 2339B, or 2339C of this title (relating to terrorism); or

(r) any conspiracy to commit any offense described in any subparagraph of this paragraph.

. . . .

**Amendments Made By Section 202 of USA PATRIOT Act
(amendments in bold text)**
18 U.S.C. § 2516. Authorization for interception of wire, oral, or
electronic communications

(1) The Attorney General, Deputy Attorney General, Associate
Attorney General, or any Assistant Attorney General, any acting Assistant Attorney General, or any Deputy Assistant Attorney General
or acting Deputy Assistant Attorney General in the Criminal Division specially designated by the Attorney General, may authorize an
application to a Federal judge of competent jurisdiction for, and such
judge may grant in conformity with section 2518 of this chapter an
order authorizing or approving the interception of wire or oral communications by the Federal Bureau of Investigation, or a Federal
agency having responsibility for the investigation of the offense as
to which the application is made, when such interception may provide or has provided evidence of—
. . . .

(c) any offense which is punishable under the following sections of this title: section 201 (bribery of public officials and witnesses), section 215 (relating to bribery of bank officials), section
224 (bribery in sporting contests), subsection (d), (e), (f), (g), (h), or
(i) of section 844 (unlawful use of explosives), section 1032 (relating to concealment of assets), section 1084 (transmission of wagering information), section 751 (relating to escape), section 1014 (relating to loans and credit applications generally; renewals and discounts), sections 1503, 1512, and 1513 (influencing or injuring an
officer, juror, or witness generally), section 1510 (obstruction of criminal investigations), section 1511 (obstruction of State or local law
enforcement), section 1751 (Presidential and Presidential staff assassination, kidnapping, and assault), section 1951 (interference with
commerce by threats or violence), section 1952 (interstate and foreign travel or transportation in aid of racketeering enterprises), section 1958 (relating to use of interstate commerce facilities in the
commission of murder for hire), section 1959 (relating to violent
crimes in aid of racketeering activity), section 1954 (offer, acceptance, or solicitation to influence operations of employee benefit

plan), section 1955 (prohibition of business enterprises of gambling), section 1956 (laundering of monetary instruments), section 1957 (relating to engaging in monetary transactions in property derived from specified unlawful activity), section 659 (theft from interstate shipment), section 664 (embezzlement from pension and welfare funds), section 1343 (fraud by wire, radio, or television), section 1344 (relating to bank fraud), sections 2251 and 2252 (sexual exploitation of children), sections 2312, 2313, 2314, and 2315 (interstate transportation of stolen property), section 2321 (relating to trafficking in certain motor vehicles or motor vehicle parts), section 1203 (relating to hostage taking), section 1029 (relating to fraud and related activity in connection with access devices), section 3146 (relating to penalty for failure to appear), section 3521 (b)(3) (relating to witness relocation and assistance), section 32 (relating to destruction of aircraft or aircraft facilities), section 38 (relating to aircraft parts fraud), section 1963 (violations with respect to racketeer influenced and corrupt organizations), section 115 (relating to threatening or retaliating against a Federal official), ~~and~~ section 1341 (relating to mail fraud)**, a felony violation of section 1030 (relating to computer fraud and abuse)**, section 351 (violations with respect to congressional, Cabinet, or Supreme Court assassinations, kidnapping, and assault), section 831 (relating to prohibited transactions involving nuclear materials), section 33 (relating to destruction of motor vehicles or motor vehicle facilities), section 175 (relating to biological weapons), section 1992 (relating to wrecking trains), a felony violation of section 1028 (relating to production of false identification documentation), section 1425 (relating to the procurement of citizenship or nationalization unlawfully), section 1426 (relating to the reproduction of naturalization or citizenship papers), section 1427 (relating to the sale of naturalization or citizenship papers), section 1541 (relating to passport issuance without authority), section 1542 (relating to false statements in passport applications), section 1543 (relating to forgery or false use of passports), section 1544 (relating to misuse of passports), or section 1546 (relating to fraud and misuse of visas, permits, and other documents);

. . . .

Amendments Made By Section 203(b) of USA PATRIOT Act
(amendments in bold text)
18 U.S.C. § 2510. Definitions
As used in this chapter—
. . . .

(19) "foreign intelligence information", for purposes of section 2517 (6) of this title, means—
(A) information, whether or not concerning a United States person, that relates to the ability of the United States to protect against—
(i) actual or potential attack or other grave hostile acts of a foreign power or an agent of a foreign power;
(ii) sabotage or international terrorism by a foreign power or an agent of a foreign power; or
(iii) clandestine intelligence activities by an intelligence service or network of a foreign power or by an agent of a foreign power; or
(B) information, whether or not concerning a United States person, with respect to a foreign power or foreign territory that relates to—
(i) the national defense or the security of the United States; or
(ii) the conduct of the foreign affairs of the United States;
. . . .

18 U.S.C. § 2517. Authorization for disclosure and use of intercepted wire, oral, or electronic communications
. . . .

(6) Any investigative or law enforcement officer, or attorney for the Government, who by any means authorized by this chapter, has obtained knowledge of the contents of any wire, oral, or electronic communication, or evidence derived therefrom, may disclose such contents to any other Federal law enforcement, intelligence, protective, immigration, national defense, or national security official to the extent that such con-

tents include foreign intelligence or counterintelligence (as defined in section 3 of the National Security Act of 1947 (50 U.S.C. 401a)), or foreign intelligence information (as defined in subsection (19) of section 2510 of this title), to assist the official who is to receive that information in the performance of his official duties. Any Federal official who receives information pursuant to this provision may use that information only as necessary in the conduct of that person's official duties subject to any limitations on the unauthorized disclosure of such information.

. . . .

Amendments Made By Section 203(d) of USA PATRIOT Act
(amendments in bold text)
50 USC § 403–5d. Foreign intelligence information

(1) In general. Notwithstanding any other provision of law, it shall be lawful for foreign intelligence or counterintelligence (as defined in section 401a of this title) or foreign intelligence information obtained as part of a criminal investigation to be disclosed to any Federal law enforcement, intelligence, protective, immigration, national defense, or national security official in order to assist the official receiving that information in the performance of his official duties. Any Federal official who receives information pursuant to this provision may use that information only as necessary in the conduct of that person's official duties subject to any limitations on the unauthorized disclosure of such information.

(2) Definition. In this section, the term "foreign intelligence information" means—

(A) information, whether or not concerning a United States person, that relates to the ability of the United States to protect against—

(i) actual or potential attack or other grave hostile acts of a foreign power or an agent of a foreign power;

(ii) sabotage or international terrorism by a foreign power or an agent of a foreign power; or

(iii) clandestine intelligence activities by an intelligence service or network of a foreign power or by an agent of a foreign power; or

(B) information, whether or not concerning a United States person, with respect to a foreign power or foreign territory that relates to—

(i) the national defense or the security of the United States; or

(ii) the conduct of the foreign affairs of the United States.

Appendix

Amendments Made By Section 204 of USA PATRIOT Act
(amendments in bold text)

18 U.S.C. § 2511. Interception and disclosure of wire, oral, or electronic communications prohibited

. . . .

(2)

. . . .

(f) Nothing contained in this chapter or chapter 121 **or 206** of this title, or section 705 of the Communications Act of 1934, shall be deemed to affect the acquisition by the United States Government of foreign intelligence information from international or foreign communications, or foreign intelligence activities conducted in accordance with otherwise applicable Federal law involving a foreign electronic communications system, utilizing a means other than electronic surveillance as defined in section 101 of the Foreign Intelligence Surveillance Act of 1978, and procedures in this chapter or chapter 121 and the Foreign Intelligence Surveillance Act of 1978 shall be the exclusive means by which electronic surveillance, as defined in section 101 of such Act, and the interception of domestic wire, **oral, and electronic** communications may be conducted.

. . . .

173

Amendments Made By Section 206 of USA PATRIOT Act
(amendments in bold text)

50 U.S.C. § 1805. Issuance of order

. . . .

(c) Specifications and directions of orders An order approving an electronic surveillance under this section shall—

. . . .

    (2) direct—

      (A) that the minimization procedures be followed;

      (B) that, upon the request of the applicant, a specified communication or other common carrier, landlord, custodian, or other specified person, **or in circumstances where the Court finds that the actions of the target of the application may have the effect of thwarting the identification of a specified person, such other persons,** furnish the applicant forthwith all information, facilities, or technical assistance necessary to accomplish the electronic surveillance in such a manner as will protect its secrecy and produce a minimum of interference with the services that such carrier, landlord, custodian, or other person is providing that target of electronic surveillance;

. . . .

Appendix

Amendments Made By Section 207 of USA PATRIOT Act
(amendments in bold text)

50 U.S.C. § 1805. Issuance of order

. . . .

(e) Duration of order; extensions; review of circumstances under which information was acquired, retained or disseminated

(1) An order issued under this section may approve an electronic surveillance for the period necessary to achieve its purpose, or for ninety days, whichever is less, except that

(A) an order under this section shall approve an electronic surveillance targeted against a foreign power, as defined in section 1801 (a)(1), (2), or (3) of this title, for the period specified in the application or for one year, whichever is less, **and**

(B) an order under this chapter for a surveillance targeted against an agent of a foreign power, as defined in section 1801 (b)(1)(A) of this title may be for the period specified in the application or for 120 days, whichever is less.

(2) Extensions of an order issued under this subchapter may be granted on the same basis as an original order upon an application for an extension and new findings made in the same manner as required for an original order, except that

(A) an extension of an order under this chapter for a surveillance targeted against a foreign power, as defined in section 1801 (a)(5) or (6) of this title, or against a foreign power as defined in section 1801 (a)(4) of this title that is not a United States person, may be for a period not to exceed one year if the judge finds probable cause to believe that no communication of any individual United States person will be acquired during the period, **and**

(B) an extension of an order under this chapter for a surveillance targeted against an agent of a foreign power as defined in section 1801 (b)(1)(A) of this title may be for a period not to exceed 1 year.

. . . .

50 U.S.C. § 1824. Issuance of order

. . . .

(d) Duration of order; extensions; assessment of compliance

(1) An order issued under this section may approve a physical search for the period necessary to achieve its purpose, or for **90 days**, whichever is less, except that

(A) an order under this section shall approve a physical search targeted against a foreign power, as defined in paragraph (1), (2), or (3) of section 1801 (a) of this title, for the period specified in the application or for one year, whichever is less**, and**

(B) an order under this section for a physical search targeted against an agent of a foreign power as defined in section 1801 (b)(1)(A) of this title may be for the period specified in the application or for 120 days, whichever is less.

(2) Extensions of an order issued under this subchapter may be granted on the same basis as the original order upon an application for an extension and new findings made in the same manner as required for the original order, except that an extension of an order under this chapter for a physical search targeted against a foreign power, as defined in section 1801 (a)(5) or (6) of this title, or against a foreign power, as defined in section 1801 (a)(4) of this title, that is not a United States person**, or against an agent of a foreign power as defined in section 1801 (b)(1)(A) of this title**, may be for a period not to exceed one year if the judge finds probable cause to believe that no property of any individual United States person will be acquired during the period.

. . . .

Amendments Made By Section 209 of USA PATRIOT Act
(amendments in bold text)

18 U.S.C. § 2510. Definitions
As used in this chapter—

(1) "wire communication" means any aural transfer made in whole or in part through the use of facilities for the transmission of communications by the aid of wire, cable, or other like connection between the point of origin and the point of reception (including the use of such connection in a switching station) furnished or operated by any person engaged in providing or operating such facilities for the transmission of interstate or foreign communications or communications affecting interstate or foreign commerce ~~and such term includes any electronic storage of such communication~~;

(14) "electronic communications system" means any wire, radio, electromagnetic, photooptical or photoelectronic facilities for the transmission of **wire or** electronic communications, and any computer facilities or related electronic equipment for the electronic storage of such communications;

18 U.S.C. § 2703. Required disclosure of customer communications or records

(a) Contents of **Wire or** Electronic Communications in Electronic Storage.— A governmental entity may require the disclosure by a provider of electronic communication service of the contents of a **wire or** electronic communication, that is in electronic storage in an electronic communications system for one hundred and eighty days or less, only pursuant to a warrant issued using the procedures described in the Federal Rules of Criminal Procedure by a court with jurisdiction over the offense under investigation or equivalent State warrant. A governmental entity may require the disclosure by a provider of electronic communications services of the contents of a **wire or** electronic communication that has been in electronic storage in an electronic communications system for more than one hundred and eighty days by the means available under subsection (b) of this section.

(b) Contents of **Wire or** Electronic Communications in a Remote Computing Service.—

(1) A governmental entity may require a provider of remote computing service to disclose the contents of any **wire or** electronic communication to which this paragraph is made applicable by paragraph (2) of this subsection—

. . . .

(2) Paragraph (1) is applicable with respect to any **wire or** electronic communication that is held or maintained on that service—

. . . .

Amendments Made By Section 212 of USA PATRIOT Act
(amendments in bold text)

18 U.S.C. § 2702. **Voluntary disclosure of customer communications or records**

(a) Prohibitions.— Except as provided in subsection (b)—

(1) a person or entity providing an electronic communication service to the public shall not knowingly divulge to any person or entity the contents of a communication while in electronic storage by that service; and

(2) a person or entity providing remote computing service to the public shall not knowingly divulge to any person or entity the contents of any communication which is carried or maintained on that service—

(A) on behalf of, and received by means of electronic transmission from (or created by means of computer processing of communications received by means of electronic transmission from), a subscriber or customer of such service; ~~and~~

(B) solely for the purpose of providing storage or computer processing services to such subscriber or customer, if the provider is not authorized to access the contents of any such communications for purposes of providing any services other than storage or computer processing; **and**

(3) a provider of remote computing service or electronic communication service to the public shall not knowingly divulge a record or other information pertaining to a subscriber to or customer of such service (not including the contents of communications covered by paragraph (1) or (2)) to any governmental entity.

(b) **Exceptions for disclosure of communications.**— A provider described in subsection (a) may divulge the contents of a communication—

(1) to an addressee or intended recipient of such communication or an agent of such addressee or intended recipient;

(2) as otherwise authorized in section 2517, 2511 (2)(a), or 2703 of this title;

(3) with the lawful consent of the originator or an addressee or intended recipient of such communication, or the subscriber in the case of remote computing service;

(4) to a person employed or authorized or whose facilities are used to forward such communication to its destination;

(5) as may be necessarily incident to the rendition of the service or to the protection of the rights or property of the provider of that service;

(6) to the National Center for Missing and Exploited Children, in connection with a report submitted thereto under section 227 of the Victims of Child Abuse Act of 1990 (42 U.S.C. 13032);

(7) to a law enforcement agency—

(A) if the contents—

(i) were inadvertently obtained by the service provider; and

(ii) appear to pertain to the commission of a crime;
~~or~~

(B) if required by section 227 of the Crime Control Act of 1990; **and**

(C) if the provider reasonably believes that an emergency involving immediate danger of death or serious physical injury to any person requires disclosure of the information without delay.

(7) to a Federal, State, or local governmental entity, if the provider, in good faith, believes that an emergency involving danger of death or serious physical injury to any person requires disclosure without delay of communications relating to the emergency.

(c) Exceptions for Disclosure of Customer Records.—A provider described in subsection (a) may divulge a record or other information pertaining to a subscriber to or customer of such service (not including the contents of communications covered by subsection (a)(1) or (a)(2))—

(1) as otherwise authorized in section 2703;

(2) with the lawful consent of the customer or subscriber;

(3) as may be necessarily incident to the rendition of the service or to the protection of the rights or property of the provider of that service;

(4) to a governmental entity, if the provider reasonably believes that an emergency involving immediate danger of death or serious physical injury to any person justifies disclosure of the information; or

(5) to the National Center for Missing and Exploited Children, in connection with a report submitted thereto under section 227 of the Victims of Child Abuse Act of 1990 (42 U.S.C. 13032); or

(6) to any person other than a governmental entity.

Note: Subsections (b)(6) and (c)(5) were redesignated subsections (b)(7) and (c)(6), respectively, by Section 227 of Public Law 108-21.

Amendments Made By Section 213 of USA PATRIOT Act
(amendments in bold text)

18 U.S.C. § 3103a. Additional grounds for issuing warrant

(a) **In General.**— In addition to the grounds for issuing a warrant in section 3103 of this title, a warrant may be issued to search for and seize any property that constitutes evidence of a criminal offense in violation of the laws of the United States.

(b) **Delay.**— **With respect to the issuance of any warrant or court order under this section, or any other rule of law, to search for and seize any property or material that constitutes evidence of a criminal offense in violation of the laws of the United States, any notice required, or that may be required, to be given may be delayed if—**

(1) the court finds reasonable cause to believe that providing immediate notification of the execution of the warrant may have an adverse result (as defined in section 2705);

(2) the warrant prohibits the seizure of any tangible property, any wire or electronic communication (as defined in section 2510), or, except as expressly provided in chapter 121, any stored wire or electronic information, except where the court finds reasonable necessity for the seizure; and

(3) the warrant provides for the giving of such notice within a reasonable period of its execution, which period may thereafter be extended by the court for good cause shown.

Amendments Made By Section 214 of USA PATRIOT Act
(amendments in bold text)

50 U.S.C. § 1842. Pen registers and trap and trace devices for foreign intelligence and international terrorism investigations

    (a) Application for authorization or approval

        (1) Notwithstanding any other provision of law, the Attorney General or a designated attorney for the Government may make an application for an order or an extension of an order authorizing or approving the installation and use of a pen register or trap and trace device ~~for any investigation to gather foreign information or information concerning international terrorism~~ **for any investigation to obtain foreign intelligence information not concerning a United States person or to protect against international terrorism or clandestine intelligence activities, provided that such investigation of a United States person is not conducted solely upon the basis of activities protected by the first amendment to the Constitution** which is being conducted by the Federal Bureau of Investigation under such guidelines as the Attorney General approves pursuant to Executive Order No. 12333, or a successor order.

   . . . .

    (c) Executive approval; contents of application Each application under this section shall require the approval of the Attorney General, or a designated attorney for the Government, and shall include—

   . . . .

        (2) a certification by the applicant that the information likely to be obtained is foreign intelligence information not concerning a United States person or is relevant to an ongoing investigation to protect against international terrorism or clandestine intelligence activities, provided that such investigation of a United States person is not conducted solely upon the basis of activities protected by the first amendment to the Constitution.

(3) information which demonstrates that there is reason to
believe that the telephone line to which the pen register or trap
and trace device is to be attached, or the communication in-
strument or device to be covered by the pen register or trap and
trace device, has been or is about to be used in communication
with—

(A) an individual who is engaging or has engaged in
international terrorism or clandestine intelligence activities that involve or may involve a violation of the criminal
laws of the United States; or

(B) a foreign power or agent of a foreign power under
circumstances giving reason to believe that the communication concerns or concerned international terrorism or
clandestine intelligence activities that involve or may involve a violation of the criminal laws of the United States.

(d) Ex parte judicial order of approval

. . . .

(2) An order issued under this section—

(A) shall specify—

(i) the identity, if known, of the person who is the subject of the investigation;

(ii) the identity, if known, of the person to whom is leased
or in whose name is listed the telephone line or other facility to which the pen register or trap and trace device is to
be attached or applied;

(iii) the attributes of the communications to which the
order applies, such as the number or other identifier, and,
if known, the location of the telephone line or other facility
to which the pen register or trap and trace device is to be
attached or applied and, in the case of a trap and trace device, the geographic limits of the trap and trace order.

. . . .

50 U.S.C. § 1843. Authorization during emergencies

(a) Requirements for authorization Notwithstanding any other
provision of this subchapter, when the Attorney General makes a

determination described in subsection (b) of this section, the Attorney General may authorize the installation and use of a pen register or trap and trace device on an emergency basis to gather ~~foreign intelligence information or information concerning international terrorism~~ foreign intelligence information not concerning a United States person or information to protect against international terrorism or clandestine intelligence activities, provided that such investigation of a United States person is not conducted solely upon the basis of activities protected by the first amendment to the Constitution if—

. . . .

(b) Determination of emergency and factual basis A determination under this subsection is a reasonable determination by the Attorney General that—

(1) an emergency requires the installation and use of a pen register or trap and trace device to obtain ~~foreign intelligence information or information concerning international terrorism~~ foreign intelligence information not concerning a United States person or information to protect against international terrorism or clandestine intelligence activities, provided that such investigation of a United States person is not conducted solely upon the basis of activities protected by the first amendment to the Constitution before an order authorizing the installation and use of the pen register or trap and trace device, as the case may be, can with due diligence be obtained under section 1842 of this title; and

. . . .

Amendments Made By Section 215 of USA PATRIOT Act
(amendments in bold text)
50 U.S.C. § 1861. Access to certain business records for foreign intelligence and international terrorism investigations

(a) Application for order; conduct of investigation generally

(1) The Director of the Federal Bureau of Investigation or a designee of the Director (whose rank shall be no lower than Assistant Special Agent in Charge) may make an application for an order requiring the production of any tangible things (including books, records, papers, documents, and other items) for an investigation to obtain foreign intelligence information not concerning a United States person or to protect against international terrorism or clandestine intelligence activities, provided that such investigation of a United States person is not conducted solely upon the basis of activities protected by the first amendment to the Constitution.

(2) An investigation conducted under this section shall—

(A) be conducted under guidelines approved by the Attorney General under Executive Order 12333 (or a successor order); and

(B) not be conducted of a United States person solely upon the basis of activities protected by the first amendment to the Constitution of the United States.

(b) Recipient and contents of application Each application under this section—

(1) shall be made to—

(A) a judge of the court established by section 1803 (a) of this title; or

(B) a United States Magistrate Judge under chapter 43 of title 28, who is publicly designated by the Chief Justice of the United States to have the power to hear applications and grant orders for the production of tangible things under this section on behalf of a judge of that court; and

(2) shall specify that the records concerned are sought for an authorized investigation conducted in accordance with subsection (a)(2) of this section to obtain foreign intelligence information not concerning a United States person or to protect against international terrorism or clandestine intelligence activities.

(c) Ex parte judicial order of approval

(1) Upon an application made pursuant to this section, the judge shall enter an ex parte order as requested, or as modified, approving the release of records if the judge finds that the application meets the requirements of this section.

(2) An order under this subsection shall not disclose that it is issued for purposes of an investigation described in subsection (a) of this section.

(d) Nondisclosure No person shall disclose to any other person (other than those persons necessary to produce the tangible things under this section) that the Federal Bureau of Investigation has sought or obtained tangible things under this section.

(e) Liability for good faith disclosure; waiver A person who, in good faith, produces tangible things under an order pursuant to this section shall not be liable to any other person for such production. Such production shall not be deemed to constitute a waiver of any privilege in any other proceeding or context.

50 USC § 1862. Congressional oversight

(a) On a semiannual basis, the Attorney General shall fully inform the Permanent Select Committee on Intelligence of the House of Representatives and the Select Committee on Intelligence of the Senate concerning all requests for the production of tangible things under section 1861 of this title.

(b) On a semiannual basis, the attorney general shall provide to the committees on the judiciary of the House of Representatives and the Senate a report setting forth with respect to the preceding 6-month period—

(1) the total number of applications made for orders approving requests for the production of tangible things under section 1861 of this title; and

(2) the total number of such orders either granted, modified, or denied."

Amendments Made By Section 217 of USA PATRIOT Act (amendments in bold text)

18 U.S.C. § 2510. Definitions

As used in this chapter—

. . . .

(18) "aural transfer" means a transfer containing the human voice at any point between and including the point of origin and the point of reception; ~~and~~

(19) "foreign intelligence information", for purposes of section 2517 (6) of this title, means—

    (A) information, whether or not concerning a United States person, that relates to the ability of the United States to protect against—

        (i) actual or potential attack or other grave hostile acts of a foreign power or an agent of a foreign power;

        (ii) sabotage or international terrorism by a foreign power or an agent of a foreign power; or

        (iii) clandestine intelligence activities by an intelligence service or network of a foreign power or by an agent of a foreign power; or

    (B) information, whether or not concerning a United States person, with respect to a foreign power or foreign territory that relates to—

        (i) the national defense or the security of the United States; or

        (ii) the conduct of the foreign affairs of the United States;

(20) "protected computer" has the meaning set forth in section 1030; and

(21) "computer trespasser"—

    (A) means a person who accesses a protected computer without authorization and thus has no reasonable expectation of privacy in any communication transmitted to, through, or from the protected computer; and

    (B) does not include a person known by the owner or

operator of the protected computer to have an existing contractual relationship with the owner or operator of the protected computer for access to all or part of the protected computer.

. . . .

18 U.S.C. § 2511. Interception and disclosure of wire, oral, or electronic communications prohibited

. . . .

(2)

(a)

(i) It shall not be unlawful under this chapter for a person acting under color of law to intercept the wire or electronic communications of a computer trespasser transmitted to, through, or from the protected computer, if—

(I) the owner or operator of the protected computer authorizes the interception of the computer trespasser's communications on the protected computer;

(II) the person acting under color of law is lawfully engaged in an investigation;

(III) the person acting under color of law has reasonable grounds to believe that the contents of the computer trespasser's communications will be relevant to the investigation; and

(IV) such interception does not acquire communications other than those transmitted to or from the computer trespasser.

. . . .

Amendments Made By Section 218 of USA PATRIOT Act
(amendments in bold text)

50 U.S.C. § 1804. Applications for court orders

(a) Submission by Federal officer; approval of Attorney General; contents — Each application for an order approving electronic surveillance under this subchapter shall be made by a Federal officer in writing upon oath or affirmation to a judge having jurisdiction under section 1803 of this title. Each application shall require the approval of the Attorney General based upon his finding that it satisfies the criteria and requirements of such application as set forth in this subchapter. It shall include—

. . . .

(7) a certification or certifications by the Assistant to the President for National Security Affairs or an executive branch official or officials designated by the President from among those executive officers employed in the area of national security or defense and appointed by the President with the advice and consent of the Senate—

(A) that the certifying official deems the information sought to be foreign intelligence information;

(B) that **the a significant** purpose of the surveillance is to obtain foreign intelligence information;

. . . .

50 U.S.C. § 1823. Application for order

(a) Submission by Federal officer; approval of Attorney General; contents—Each application for an order approving a physical search under this subchapter shall be made by a Federal officer in writing upon oath or affirmation to a judge of the Foreign Intelligence Surveillance Court. Each application shall require the approval of the Attorney General based upon the Attorney General's finding that it satisfies the criteria and requirements for such application as set forth in this subchapter. Each application shall include—

. . . .

(7) a certification or certifications by the Assistant to the President for National Security Affairs or an executive branch official or officials designated by the President from among those executive branch officers employed in the area of national security or defense and appointed by the President, by and with the advice and consent of the Senate—

(A) that the certifying official deems the information sought to be foreign intelligence information;

(B) that ~~the~~ a significant purpose of the search is to obtain foreign intelligence information;

. . . .

Appendix

Amendments Made By Section 220 of USA PATRIOT Act
(amendments in bold text)

18 U.S.C. § 2703. Required disclosure of customer communications or records

(a) Contents of Wire or Electronic Communications in Electronic Storage.— A governmental entity may require the disclosure by a provider of electronic communication service of the contents of a wire or electronic communication, that is in electronic storage in an electronic communications system for one hundred and eighty days or less, only pursuant to a warrant issued ~~under the Federal Rules of Criminal Procedure~~ **using the procedures described in the Federal Rules of Criminal Procedure by a court with jurisdiction over the offense under investigation** or equivalent State warrant. A governmental entity may require the disclosure by a provider of electronic communications services of the contents of a wire or electronic communication that has been in electronic storage in an electronic communications system for more than one hundred and eighty days by the means available under subsection (b) of this section.

(b) Contents of Wire or Electronic Communications in a Remote Computing Service.—

(1) A governmental entity may require a provider of remote computing service to disclose the contents of any wire or electronic communication to which this paragraph is made applicable by paragraph (2) of this subsection—

(A) without required notice to the subscriber or customer, if the governmental entity obtains a warrant issued ~~under the Federal Rules of Criminal Procedure~~ **using the procedures described in the Federal Rules of Criminal Procedure by a court with jurisdiction over the offense under investigation** or equivalent State warrant; or

(B) with prior notice from the governmental entity to the subscriber or customer if the governmental entity—

(i) uses an administrative subpoena authorized by a Federal or State statute or a Federal or State grand

193

jury or trial subpoena; or

(ii) obtains a court order for such disclosure under subsection (d) of this section;

except that delayed notice may be given pursuant to section 2705 of this title.

(2) Paragraph (1) is applicable with respect to any wire or electronic communication that is held or maintained on that service—

(A) on behalf of, and received by means of electronic transmission from (or created by means of computer processing of communications received by means of electronic transmission from), a subscriber or customer of such remote computing service; and

(B) solely for the purpose of providing storage or computer processing services to such subscriber or customer, if the provider is not authorized to access the contents of any such communications for purposes of providing any services other than storage or computer processing.

(c) Records Concerning Electronic Communication Service or Remote Computing Service.—

(1) A governmental entity may require a provider of electronic communication service or remote computing service to disclose a record or other information pertaining to a subscriber to or customer of such service (not including the contents of communications) only when the governmental entity—

(A) obtains a warrant issued ~~under the Federal Rules of Criminal Procedure~~ **using the procedures described in the Federal Rules of Criminal Procedure by a court with jurisdiction over the offense under investigation** or equivalent State warrant;

. . . .

(d) Requirements for Court Order.— A court order for disclosure under subsection (b) or (c) may be issued by any court that is a court of competent jurisdiction ~~described in section 3127 (2)(A)~~

and shall issue only if the governmental entity offers specific and articulable facts showing that there are reasonable grounds to believe that the contents of a wire or electronic communication, or the records or other information sought, are relevant and material to an ongoing criminal investigation. In the case of a State governmental authority, such a court order shall not issue if prohibited by the law of such State. A court issuing an order pursuant to this section, on a motion made promptly by the service provider, may quash or modify such order, if the information or records requested are unusually voluminous in nature or compliance with such order otherwise would cause an undue burden on such provider.

. . . .

18 U.S.C. § 2711. Definitions for chapter
As used in this chapter—

(1) the terms defined in section 2510 of this title have, respectively, the definitions given such terms in that section; and

(2) the term "remote computing service" means the provision to the public of computer storage or processing services by means of an electronic communications system; **and**

(3) **the term "court of competent jurisdiction" has the meaning assigned by section 3127, and includes any Federal court within that definition, without geographic limitation.**

Amendments Made By Section 223 of USA PATRIOT Act
(amendments in bold text)

18 U.S.C. § 2520. Recovery of civil damages authorized

(a) In General.— Except as provided in section 2511 (2)(a)(ii), any person whose wire, oral, or electronic communication is intercepted, disclosed, or intentionally used in violation of this chapter may in a civil action recover from the person or entity, **other than the United States,** which engaged in that violation such relief as may be appropriate.

. . . .

(f) **Administrative Discipline.— If a court or appropriate department or agency determines that the United States or any of its departments or agencies has violated any provision of this chapter, and the court or appropriate department or agency finds that the circumstances surrounding the violation raise serious questions about whether or not an officer or employee of the United States acted willfully or intentionally with respect to the violation, the department or agency shall, upon receipt of a true and correct copy of the decision and findings of the court or appropriate department or agency promptly initiate a proceeding to determine whether disciplinary action against the officer or employee is warranted. If the head of the department or agency involved determines that disciplinary action is not warranted, he or she shall notify the Inspector General with jurisdiction over the department or agency concerned and shall provide the Inspector General with the reasons for such determination.**

(g) **Improper Disclosure Is Violation.— Any willful disclosure or use by an investigative or law enforcement officer or governmental entity of information beyond the extent permitted by section 2517 is a violation of this chapter for purposes of section 2520 (a).**

18 U.S.C. § 2707. Civil action

(a) Cause of Action.— Except as provided in section 2703 (e), any provider of electronic communication service, subscriber, or other person aggrieved by any violation of this chapter in which the conduct constituting the violation is engaged in with a knowing or intentional state of mind may, in a civil action, recover from the person or entity, **other than the United States,** which engaged in that violation such relief as may be appropriate.

. . . .

(d) Administrative Discipline.—If a court or appropriate department or agency determines that the United States or any of its departments or agencies has violated any provision of this chapter, and the court or appropriate department or agency finds that the circumstances surrounding the violation raise serious questions about whether or not an officer or employee of the United States acted willfully or intentionally with respect to the violation, the department or agency shall, upon receipt of a true and correct copy of the decision and findings of the court or appropriate department or agency promptly initiate a proceeding to determine whether disciplinary action against the officer or employee is warranted. If the head of the department or agency involved determines that disciplinary action is not warranted, he or she shall notify the Inspector General with jurisdiction over the department or agency concerned and shall provide the Inspector General with the reasons for such determination.

. . . .

(g) Improper Disclosure.—Any willful disclosure of a "record", as that term is defined in section 552a (a) of title 5, United States Code, obtained by an investigative or law enforcement officer, or a governmental entity, pursuant to section 2703 of this title, or from a device installed pursuant to section 3123 or 3125 of this title, that is not a disclosure made in the proper performance of the official functions of the officer or governmental entity making the disclosure, is a violation of this chapter. This provision shall not apply to information previously lawfully disclosed (prior to the commencement of any civil or

administrative proceeding under this chapter) to the public by a Federal, State, or local governmental entity or by the plaintiff in a civil action under this chapter.

18 U.S.C. § 2712. Civil actions against the United States

(a) In General.— Any person who is aggrieved by any willful violation of this chapter or of chapter 119 of this title or of sections 106(a), 305(a), or 405(a) of the Foreign Intelligence Surveillance Act of 1978 (50 U.S.C. 1801 et seq.) may commence an action in United States District Court against the United States to recover money damages. In any such action, if a person who is aggrieved successfully establishes such a violation of this chapter or of chapter 119 of this title or of the above specific provisions of title 50, the Court may assess as damages—

(1) actual damages, but not less than $10,000, whichever amount is greater; and

(2) litigation costs, reasonably incurred.

(b) Procedures.—

(1) Any action against the United States under this section may be commenced only after a claim is presented to the appropriate department or agency under the procedures of the Federal Tort Claims Act, as set forth in title 28, United States Code.

(2) Any action against the United States under this section shall be forever barred unless it is presented in writing to the appropriate Federal agency within 2 years after such claim accrues or unless action is begun within 6 months after the date of mailing, by certified or registered mail, of notice of final denial of the claim by the agency to which it was presented. The claim shall accrue on the date upon which the claimant first has a reasonable opportunity to discover the violation.

(3) Any action under this section shall be tried to the court without a jury.

(4) Notwithstanding any other provision of law, the procedures set forth in section 106(f), 305(g), or 405(f) of the Foreign Intelligence Surveillance Act of 1978 (50 U.S.C. 1801 et seq.) shall be the exclusive means by which materials governed by those sections may be reviewed.

(5) An amount equal to any award against the United States under this section shall be reimbursed by the department or agency concerned to the fund described in section 1304 of title 31, United States Code, out of any appropriation, fund, or other account (excluding any part of such appropriation, fund, or account that is available for the enforcement of any Federal law) that is available for the operating expenses of the department or agency concerned.

(c) Administrative Discipline.— If a court or appropriate department or agency determines that the United States or any of its departments or agencies has violated any provision of this chapter, and the court or appropriate department or agency finds that the circumstances surrounding the violation raise serious questions about whether or not an officer or employee of the United States acted willfully or intentionally with respect to the violation, the department or agency shall, upon receipt of a true and correct copy of the decision and findings of the court or appropriate department or agency promptly initiate a proceeding to determine whether disciplinary action against the officer or employee is warranted. If the head of the department or agency involved determines that disciplinary action is not warranted, he or she shall notify the Inspector General with jurisdiction over the department or agency concerned and shall provide the Inspector General with the reasons for such determination.

(d) Exclusive Remedy.— Any action against the United States under this subsection shall be the exclusive remedy against the United States for any claims within the purview of this section.

(e) Stay of Proceedings.—

(1) Upon the motion of the United States, the court shall stay any action commenced under this section if the court determines that civil discovery will adversely affect the ability of the Government to conduct a related investigation or the prosecution of a related criminal case. Such a stay shall toll the limitations periods of paragraph (2) of subsection (b).

(2) In this subsection, the terms "related criminal case" and "related investigation" mean an actual prosecution or investigation in progress at the time at which the request for the stay or any subsequent motion to lift the stay is made. In determining whether an investigation or a criminal case is related to an action commenced under this section, the court shall consider the degree of similarity between the parties, witnesses, facts, and circumstances involved in the 2 proceedings, without requiring that any one or more factors be identical.

(3) In requesting a stay under paragraph (1), the Government may, in appropriate cases, submit evidence ex parte in order to avoid disclosing any matter that may adversely affect a related investigation or a related criminal case. If the Government makes such an ex parte submission, the plaintiff shall be given an opportunity to make a submission to the court, not ex parte, and the court may, in its discretion, request further information from either party.

Amendments Made By Section 225 of USA PATRIOT Act
(amendments in bold text)

50 U.S.C. § 1805. Issuance of order

. . . .

(h) Bar to legal action No cause of action shall lie in any court against any provider of a wire or electronic communication service, landlord, custodian, or other person (including any officer, employee, agent, or other specified person thereof) that furnishes any information, facilities, or technical assistance in accordance with a court order or request for emergency assistance under this chapter for electronic surveillance or physical search.

Note: Subsection (h) was redesignated subsection (i) by Section 314 of Public Law 107-108.

Amendments Made By Section 805 of USA PATRIOT Act
(amendments in bold text)

18 U.S.C. § 2339A. Providing material support to terrorists

(a) Offense.— Whoever ~~within the United States~~ provides material support or resources or conceals or disguises the nature, location, source, or ownership of material support or resources, knowing or intending that they are to be used in preparation for, or in carrying out, a violation of section 32, 37, 81, 175, **229,** 351, 831, 842 (m) or (n), 844 (f) or (i), 930 (c), 956, 1114, 1116, 1203, 1361, 1362, 1363, 1366, 1751, 1992, **1993,** 2155, 2156, 2280, 2281, 2332, 2332a, 2332b, 2332f, or 2340A of this title, **section 236 of the Atomic Energy Act of 1954 (42 U.S.C. 2284),** or section 46502 **or 60123 (b)** of title 49, or in preparation for, or in carrying out, the concealment of an escape from the commission of any such violation, or attempts or conspires to do such an act, shall be fined under this title, imprisoned not more than 15 years, or both, and, if the death of any person results, shall be imprisoned for any term of years or for life. **A violation of this section may be prosecuted in any Federal judicial district in which the underlying offense was committed, or in any other Federal judicial district as provided by law.**

(b) Definition.— In this section, the term "material support or resources" means currency or ~~other financial securities~~ **monetary instruments or financial securities,** financial services, lodging, training, **expert advice or assistance,** safehouses, false documentation or identification, communications equipment, facilities, weapons, lethal substances, explosives, personnel, transportation, and other physical assets, except medicine or religious materials.

18 U.S.C. § 1956. Laundering of monetary instruments

(c) As used in this section—

. . . .

(7) the term "specified unlawful activity" means—

. . . .

(D) an offense under section 32 (relating to the destruction of aircraft), section 37 (relating to violence at international airports), section 115 (relating to influencing, impeding, or retaliating against a Federal official by threatening or injuring a family member), section 152 (relating to concealment of assets; false oaths and claims; bribery), section 215 (relating to commissions or gifts for procuring loans), section 351 (relating to congressional or Cabinet officer assassination), any of sections 500 through 503 (relating to certain counterfeiting offenses), section 513 (relating to securities of States and private entities), section 541 (relating to goods falsely classified), section 542 (relating to entry of goods by means of false statements), section 545 (relating to smuggling goods into the United States), section 549 (relating to removing goods from Customs custody), section 641 (relating to public money, property, or records), section 656 (relating to theft, embezzlement, or misapplication by bank officer or employee), section 657 (relating to lending, credit, and insurance institutions), section 658 (relating to property mortgaged or pledged to farm credit agencies), section 666 (relating to theft or bribery concerning programs receiving Federal funds), section 793, 794, or 798 (relating to espionage), section 831 (relating to prohibited transactions involving nuclear materials), section 844 (f) or (i) (relating to destruction by explosives or fire of Government property or property affecting interstate or foreign commerce), section 875 (relating to interstate communications), section 922 (l) (relating to the unlawful importation of firearms), section 924 (n) (relating to firearms trafficking), section 956 (relating to conspiracy to kill, kidnap, maim, or injure certain property in a foreign country), section 1005 (relating to fraudulent bank entries), 1006 (relating to fraudulent Federal credit institution entries), 1007 (relating to Federal Deposit Insurance transactions), 1014 (relating to fraudulent loan or credit applications), section 1030 (relating to computer fraud and abuse), 1032 (relating to concealment of assets from conservator, receiver, or liquidating agent of financial institution), section 1111 (relating to murder), section 1114 (relating to murder of United States law enforcement officials), section 1116 (relating to murder of foreign officials, official guests, or internationally protected persons), section 1201 (relating to kidnapping), section 1203 (relating to hostage taking), section 1361 (relating to willful injury of Government property), section 1363 (relating to destruction of property within the special maritime and territorial jurisdiction), section 1708 (theft from the mail), section 1751 (relating to Presidential assassination), section 2113 or 2114 (relating to bank and postal robbery and theft), section 2280 (relating to violence against maritime navigation), section 2281 (relating to violence against maritime fixed platforms), section 2319 (relating to copyright infringement), section 2320 (relating to trafficking in counterfeit goods and services), section 2332 (relating to terrorist acts abroad against United States nationals), section 2332a (relating to use of weapons of mass destruction), section 2332b (relating to international terrorist acts transcending national boundaries), or section 2339A **or 2339B** (relating to providing material support to terrorists) of this title, section 46502 of title 49, United States Code, a felony violation of the Chemical Diversion and Trafficking Act of 1988 (relating to precursor and essential chemicals), section 590 of the Tariff Act of 1930 (19 U.S.C. 1590) (relating to aviation smuggling), section 422 of the Controlled Substances Act (relating to transportation of drug paraphernalia), section 38 (c) (relating to criminal violations) of the Arms Export Control Act, section 11 (relating to violations) of the Export Administration Act of 1979, section 206 (relating to penalties) of the International Emergency Economic Powers Act, section 16 (relating to offenses and punishment) of the Trading with the Enemy Act, any felony violation of section 15 of the Food Stamp Act of 1977 (relating to food stamp fraud) involving a quantity of coupons having a value of not less than $5,000, any violation of section 543(a)(1) of the Housing Act of 1949 (relating to equity skimming), any felony violation of the Foreign Agents Registration Act of 1938, or any felony violation of the Foreign Corrupt Practices Act; environmental crimes

Amendments Made By Section 6001 of the Intelligence Reform and Terrorism Prevention Act of 2004 Act (amendments in bold text)

50 U.S.C. § 1801. Definitions

As used in this subchapter:

(b) "Agent of a foreign power" means—

(1) any person other than a United States person, who—

. . . .

(C) engages in international terrorism or activities in preparation therefore; or

. . . .

Table of Cases